MW00489030

THE WASHING
OF THE
SAINTS' FEET

J. MATTHEW
PINSON

THE WASHING OF THE SAINTS' FEET

J. MATTHEW PINSON

Randall House Publications
114 Bush Road • PO Box 17306
Nashville, TN 37217 USA
www.RandallHouse.com

THE WASHING OF THE SAINTS' FEET
BY J. MATTHEW PINSON

Published by Randall House Publications
114 Bush Road
Nashville, Tennessee 37217

Printed in the United States of America
ISBN 0892655224
Library of Congress Control Number: 2006926919
Library of Congress Cataloging-in-Publication Data

Pinson, J. Matthew, 1967-
  The washing of the saints' feet / J. Matthew Pinson.
    p. cm.
  Includes bibliographical references and index.
  ISBN 0-89265-522-4
1. Foot washing (Rite)--History of doctrines. I. Title.

BV873.F7P56 2006
265'.9--dc22

2006018185

TABLE OF CONTENTS

I lovingly dedicate this book
to my parents,

JOHN AND LINDA PINSON,

who faithfully took me
to the washing of the saints' feet
and instilled in me a love for it.

FOREWORD

It is interesting to observe that in spite of the fact that the majority of denominations do not practice washing the saints' feet, the practice is still with us. Some, who agree that in John 13:1-15 Jesus instituted feet washing to be practiced by His followers still seem to be reluctant about observing the rite. They seem to think there is a problem with the way it may be perceived. If the church observes the rite of feet washing, they are not sure that a strong church can be built in today's culture. But in spite of all that has been said to discredit it, feet washing is still being observed by many. No one has ever been able to come up with a knockout blow that would give feet washing a place among the relics of the past. It may be a little early to say this, but I believe there may be a trend for feet washing to gain more acceptance as a rite to be practiced.

J. Matthew Pinson has done all of us a favor by dealing with this subject in *The Washing of the Saints' Feet*. He is well qualified in his experience to deal with this subject. He comes from a family of devout Christians, who places great value on the church ordinances. His grandfather, the Reverend L. V. Pinson, a Free Will Baptist minister, was the pastor of his home church. This family had good rapport with other evangelical Christians, but they also had a deep appreciation for the traditions of Free Will Baptists.

Pinson has had a very broad educational experience, having done undergraduate study at Free Will Baptist Bible College and graduate study at the University of West Florida, Yale University, Florida State University, and Regent College, Vancouver. He is currently pursuing a doctorate at Vanderbilt University. He has had broad experience as a pastor and has served as the president of Free Will Baptist Bible College since 2002. He is the author of *A Free Will Baptist Handbook: Heritage, Beliefs, and Ministries*, (Nashville: Randall House, 1998). He invited four biblical scholars to write on the subject of the security of the believer and edited the book, *Four Views of Eternal Security*, (Grand Rapids: Zondervan, 2002).

Pinson is an avid reader. Not only is he well aware of the problems facing the church today, but he also has an appreciation for the Scripture-based and time-honored traditions of the past. *The Washing of the Saints' Feet* addresses one of his loves and deep concerns—the ordinance of feet washing.

In this book Pinson addresses a wide variety of problems that people now raise and have raised in the history of the church concerning feet washing. Among those who believe that feet washing should be practiced, some have had reservations about whether it should be called an ordinance. Pinson gives a great deal of attention to the distinction between the words *ordinance* and *sacrament*. His treatment of how the use of these terms reflects the various theological traditions is very informative. This knowledge alone would make the book worth reading. Pinson gives a very strong defense of the position supporting feet washing as an ordinance. He comes at the subject from almost every angle, while dealing with the subject from the side of biblical interpretation.

The Washing of the Saints' Feet deserves to be read broadly and critically. It is a good book to be used in a group study where the members want to examine the evidence and think through the issues.

Pinson's knowledge of church history as well as his ability to think critically and write with clarity makes this a book that will benefit anyone, regardless of academic credentials. It is a must read for those who want to be informed on the subject of feet washing, no matter what their convictions may be.

May God's blessings be upon *The Washing of the Saints' Feet* and those who read it, giving critical thought to the question of washing the saints' feet as an ordinance.

F. Leroy Forlines, Professor Emeritus of Theology

Free Will Baptist Bible College

Nashville, Tennessee

PREFACE

Of all my memories of the church, the washing of the saints' feet is among the earliest and most vivid. I remember—after a solemn searching of heart and mind and feasting reverently at the Lord's table—gathering with men and boys, old and young, to engage in the ritual of feet washing. It seemed then to me, as it seems now, one of the most meaningful experiences of my life—and yet one of the strangest. Only after I became an adult and began studying theology would I realize that the most distinguished scholars in the field of anthropology say that true religious ritual is always characterized by an oddness, a strangeness, a mystery, a separateness from the normal warp and woof of life. Yet, they say, those same rituals ring profoundly true with human beings about the depths of human experience and need.

I have come to the conclusion that much of the ritual in Christian history has no warrant in Scripture. The Bible does, however, commend to the church corporate rituals that vividly remind our senses of the grace of God in Jesus Christ. I am thinking of baptism, the Lord's Supper, the washing of the saints' feet, anointing the sick with oil, and even fasting. All of these involve the senses—tasting, touching, smelling, seeing, and hearing.

Theologians from liturgical churches often decry the Baptist and free church traditions for putting too much emphasis on the Word and not enough on images and the senses (incense, bells, icons, the sign of the cross, clerical dress, and holy water, for example). Our reply is that God reveals in Scripture everything that is necessary for life and godliness and the functioning of Christ's body.

Those rites He *has* ordained and revealed in Scripture *are* our images. They are our pictures of our trinitarian God as He condescends to our low estate in the person of His Son Jesus Christ, taking on our humanity; being crucified, buried, and raised for our justification; bringing sanctification through His Holy Spirit, who gives us healing and hope and His divine presence working through His Word. These scriptural images are the only images we need. This is another way of saying that the things God has ordained are the only things the church needs. Indeed, we could say that the rites He has ordained are means by which He gives grace to His church—means by which He shows Himself and His salvation— and they are the only means at our disposal.[1]

This book is about one of those means through which God shows Himself and His salvation to us in the context of the gathered church. Through feet washing, God symbolizes for us the meaning of the gospel, the meaning of our redemption in Christ. He symbolizes it and teaches it and explains it in a way that makes a vivid impression on us—on our minds, our hearts, our wills, and our senses.

The aim of this book is to aid in the reformation of our churches by returning to God's means of grace for the church—means that we believe, with our forebears, were taught by Christ and His apostles. I believe that a reinvestigation of the practice of feet washing and a clear understanding of *why* we should practice it will prepare the way for a renewal of the ordinance in our time.

In short, my aim in this book is to help open us up to our historic tradition of the washing of the saints' feet. My hope is that my generation can build upon the theological foundations of previous generations and launch out into radical (Latin *radix* = root, foundation) ways of living out the gospel in the communal life of our churches. I believe that the regular, ritual practice of feet washing is something that Free Will Baptists have to offer the body of Christ in the twenty-first century. To do this, we must get out from behind the shadow of other Protestant visions of the church. We must reach deep within our scriptural tradition as Free Will Baptists and mine the gems of our past. This is the only way we can hope to forge a viable and vibrant Free Will Baptist witness to Christ and His truth in the twenty-first century.

This book has its beginnings as the 2004 F. Leroy Forlines Lectures at Free Will Baptist Bible College. I was privileged when the members of the Department of Biblical and Ministry Studies at FWBBC invited their president to deliver these annual lectures. When they informed me that I could lecture on any topic, I almost immediately decided to speak on the washing of the saints' feet. The lectures were a combination of new material as well as sermons and talks I had given on the subject over several years of ministry. I also adapted portions of an article I had written for the inaugural edition of *Integrity*, the publication of the Commission for Theological Integrity of the National Association of Free Will Baptists.[2]

This book is no scholarly treatise. Rather, it is a series of lectures designed for college students and edited for print. While I have made minor changes, the substance and style of the book remain for the most part that of the lectures. Thus, I have retained contractions, colloquialisms, and other marks of informal lectures.[3]

As I intimated in the last paragraph, this is not designed as a scholarly work.[4] It bears the marks, I hope, of careful and sustained thought. Yet it is intended as only a beginning point—a foundation for scholarly work that I trust some rising young Free Will Baptist scholars will embark on in the future.

I am pleased to present as a part of this book six hymns on the washing of the saints' feet. Including these hymns illustrates my desire to tie theological thinking to thinking and acting about worship. The hymn "He Washed His Servants Feet" is from an early (and now rare) southern Free Will Baptist hymnal called *Zion's Hymns*; it is set to the same tune to which it is set in *Rejoice: The Free Will Baptist Hymn Book*. The hymn "Feet Washing" has been arranged by James M. Stevens, chairman of the Department of Music at Free Will Baptist Bible College. His arrangement is based on the original arrangement by N. P. Gates found in *The Free Will Baptist Hymnal* (1958).

The text of "The Basin and the Towel" was written by Robert E. Picirilli, Professor Emeritus and former Academic Dean at Free Will Baptist Bible College. The text of "Emblems of Thy Condescension" was written by Mary Ruth Wisehart, former English professor at Free Will Baptist Bible College and Executive Secretary-Treasurer of Women Nationally Active for Christ of the National Association of Free Will Baptists. Both of these texts were written for the *Free Will Baptist Hymn Book* (1964). All of the above hymns can be found in *Rejoice: The Free Will Baptist Hymn Book*.

The hymn "Jesus the Lord, Who Bled and Died" is both old and new. The text comes from *Zion's Hymns* but has been set to a new tune composed for this book by James Stevens. "Love Consecrates the Humblest Act" can be found in *Rejoice: The Free Will Baptist Hymn Book*. That hymn is taken from the Mennonite *Church Hymnal*, and is set to an old tune from the nineteenth-century folk song book, *Southern Harmony*. James Stevens kindly arranged that tune for this book.

I have many people to thank for their part in this work. I want to thank the Department of Biblical and Ministry Studies of Free Will Baptist Bible College for sponsoring the F. Leroy Forlines Lectures and inviting me to give them. I also want to thank my administrative assistant, Melissa Lewis, who gave invaluable aid typing the lectures. I thank James Stevens for composing a new tune for "Jesus the Lord, Who Bled and Died," arranging other tunes, and engraving and typesetting the hymns included in this book. I also owe gratitude to Leroy Forlines and Darrell Holley, long-time friends and also colleagues at FWBBC, both of whom read the manuscript and gave me helpful feedback. Lastly, I wish to thank my wife Melinda and my children Anna and Matthew. Melinda read and commented on the manuscript and gave needed encouragement for this work and its ideas. Anna and Matthew have lovingly supported their father through the writing of these lectures. May Christ receive all the glory, for it is of Him that this book speaks.

J. Matthew Pinson

NOTES

1. When I say that God gives His church "means of grace," I mean this in the broad sense used in the above paragraph when I said that God reveals in Scripture everything that is necessary for life and godliness and the functioning of Christ's body. I do not mean that the ordinances give grace in a special saving or sanctifying way that He does not give in other things such as singing praise to God, the ministry of the Word, laying on of hands, fasting, prayer, or any other practice that God gives His people for their edification. For more on this, please see chapter two.

2. J. Matthew Pinson, "Toward a Theology of the Ordinances with Special Reference to Feet Washing," *Integrity: A Journal of Christian Thought*, (Summer 2000), 67-87. Portions of the article were adapted for the lectures and are scattered throughout the book. I have also included as an appendix a section of the article that deals with the historical background of ordinances and sacraments.

3. I have designed this book so that readers who want to stay with the flow of the lecture can read the body of the text, but those who wish to dig deeper into documentation and more in-depth comments can consult the notes at the end of each chapter. Appendix Three also provides study/discussion questions for those who wish to strengthen comprehension or participate in a small group study. These study questions are available on-line at *www.RandallHouse.com*.

4. It is important for me to emphasize the limitations of this short work. It is neither a work of exegetical or systematic theology. It is more impressionistic, practical, and conversational than a work of scholarship. It comes much closer to being similar to an extended topical sermon.

INTRODUCTORY REFLECTIONS
ON
FEET WASHING

Chapter One

CHAPTER ONE

I want to be like Jesus,
His word my soul to keep.
And humbly like Him kneeling,
And wash my brother's feet.

Dear Lord, may I be a little more humble
Daily follow thee, may I not retreat.
Ere I should cause my brother to stumble,
May I humbly kneel and wash his feet.

The above verse and chorus from the song "Feet Washing" in the *Free Will Baptist Hymnal* (1958)[1] describes a ritual that is practiced in Free Will Baptist churches across the world. Feet washing is a rite that, as its practitioners realize, most outsiders view as an oddity. Sociologist John Shelton Reed, in discussing in third person his experiences as a Southern boy at MIT in the '60s, relates that, when he ran out of true stories to entertain his Yankee friends, "he was not above talking about things he only knew of second hand: swamps and alligators, foot washing and snake handling, moon shining and stock car racing. When he found a truly gullible listener, sometimes he really laid it on."[2]

Free Will Baptists, it is sure, do not make or drink moonshine. They may or may not race stock cars. And they definitely do not handle snakes.[3] However, Free Will Baptists have for almost four centuries washed feet. They believe that the washing of the saints' feet is an ordinance of the gospel that the people of God should practice in the context of the local New Testament *ekklesia*, or church.

A WIDESPREAD PRACTICE

Feet washing used to be a widespread practice among Baptists. In fact, Howard Dorgan, in his book *Giving Glory to God in Appalachia*, says that most Baptists of all stripes in Appalachia still observe the ordinance of feet washing, whether they are Missionary Baptists, Southern Baptists, Primitive Baptists, Regular Baptists—and on and on the list goes.[4] All Primitive Baptists still observe the rite, as well as a number of other groups, such as the various Churches of God,[5] Mennonites of all sorts (including Amish), Church of the Brethren, Grace Brethren,[6] and Hutterians (also known as Hutterites). Among some Wesleyans the practice persists. There are liturgies for the washing of feet in the worship books of several mainline Protestant denominations, including the Episcopal Church's *Book of Common Prayer*. Even Seventh Day Adventists practice feet washing.[7]

Several other denominations used to practice feet washing that have since done away with the ritual. For example, the early Moravians and Hussites practiced it. The early Churches of Christ, Christian churches, and Disciples of Christ, following their founder Alexander Campbell, used to observe the washing of feet, and, as I will discuss later, we see the rite of feet washing all throughout the church's history. It is well-attested in early and medieval Christianity. Someone as well known as Bernard of Clairvaux believed that the washing of the saints' feet was a sacrament, and he listed it along with the other sacraments of the medieval Catholic Church.[8]

THE FREE WILL BAPTIST HERITAGE

Free Will Baptists brought the ordinance over from seventeenth-century England, where our English General Baptist forefathers practiced it. The first Baptists, John Smyth and Thomas Helwys, apparently received the practice from the Dutch Waterlander Mennonites when they were exiled in Amsterdam in the early 1600s. The illustrious English General Baptist minister William Jeffrey of Kent refers to feet washing in his book *The Whole Faith of Man*, written in 1659. He says:

> Also, take notice of that Ordinance of Christ, of washing the Saints' feet, it is commanded by Christ, and a blessing promised to them that do it, . . . and therefore it ought to be done, and it setteth out Christ's humility, and puts us in mind of the same; so declaring that the wayes of Christ are self-denying wayes; and this is a self-denying thing, and therefore serveth to humble the creature, and to beget familiarity, and love one with another, it being done decently and in order.[9]

The *1812 Abstract* was the primary early confession of faith among Free Will Baptists in the American South, and it encapsulates the Free Will Baptist approach to feet washing. "We believe," it says,

> as touching gospel ordinances, in believer's baptism, laying on of hands, receiving the sacrament in bread and wine, washing the saints' feet, anointing the sick with oil in the name of the Lord, fasting, prayer, singing praise to God, and the public ministry of the Word, with every institution of the Lord we shall find in the New Testament.[10]

Our *Treatise of the Faith and Practices of the National Association of Free Will Baptists* affirms the washing of the saints' feet as an ordinance in three places. "The Faith of Free Will Baptists" describes feet washing as "a sacred ordinance" and says that "it is the duty and happy prerogative of every believer" to observe it.[11] The "Articles of Faith" says that feet washing is an ordinance that is "of universal obligation and is to be ministered to all true believers."[12] "The Practices of Free Will Baptists" states that "provision should be made for regular observance of the Lord's Supper and for washing of the saints' feet by the congregation."[13]

THE MEANING OF THE WORD *PREROGATIVE*

I want to correct a misinterpretation of chapter 13 in "The Faith of Free Will Baptists," where it says that it is "the duty and happy prerogative of every believer to observe this sacred ordinance." Often people who want to say that washing the saints' feet is optional and that we should no longer observe the practice have misunderstood the word *prerogative*. They have argued that, because the *Treatise* uses the word *prerogative* here, feet washing is an option—that it is one's choice.

The problem with that statement is that the word *choice* is not an accurate definition of the word *prerogative*. Standard English dictionaries define the word *prerogative* as "right or privilege." Often people today use the word to mean "a choice or an option." Yet, what the word *prerogative* actually means in this context is "right or privilege." Furthermore, that is the only usage of the word that is consistent with the word *duty*, also used in this same statement. How can something be a *duty* and yet a *choice*? Something that is your duty cannot be an option for you. The only usage of the word *prerogative* that is consistent with *duty* is the main usage throughout the history of the English language: *one's right or privilege*. So we should say that it is the duty and right or happy privilege of every believer to observe this sacred ordinance.

THE MYTH OF WESTERN NON-OBSERVANCE

There is another myth that floats around Free Will Baptists in the eastern United States: that Free Will Baptists west of the Mississippi (e.g., Arkansas, Missouri, Oklahoma, Texas, California) are less insistent on the practice of feet washing than those east of the Mississippi. I remember when I first became interested in theology and church history and began to look into this question, I heard a few people say this: Out west it is not as important for them, and they do not insist on it. But this really is a myth, as those who grew up in those states know.

The origin of this myth is probably as follows: When eastern and western Free Will Baptists began in 1918-19 to attempt to come together in a new potential national association, a few outspoken leaders in the Cooperative General Association of Free Will Baptists in the West did not practice feet washing. One of these was John H. Wolfe of Nebraska, who soon passed off the scene. He argued vehemently that the washing of the saints' feet should not be made obligatory. So the deal was off. There was no national association founded in 1919. Not until 1935 would this union take place, and feet washing as an ordinance was necessary to the union.

I thought for a number of years that this meant (and heard that this meant) Free Will Baptists west of the Mississippi were less insistent on feet washing. Later I discovered that they were just as resolute as Free Will Baptists east of the Mississippi. In fact, the Cooperative

General Association itself published a book in the 1920s that outlined their doctrine. In that book they strongly affirmed the washing of the saints' feet in connection with the Lord's Supper.

Furthermore, a survey of minutes of Oklahoma, Arkansas, and Missouri Free Will Baptist associations going back to the nineteenth century reveals some interesting facts. Not only did many of these associations not ordain anyone who was a pre-millennialist, they would also not ordain anyone who did *not* believe in the ordinance of feet washing. They would not even ordain anyone who believed that it should be practiced at any time other than at night! That is how insistent they were on the literal observance of feet washing in the ritual life of the church. The unfortunate myth of Western non-observance has floated around. Yet, a casual perusal of the documents reveals that this is not the case.

STRANGE THINGS

Free Will Baptists *confess* feet washing to be an ordinance. Why, then, are there some Free Will Baptists who no longer participate in this ritual? Most Free Will Baptists of my own generation grew up engaging in the washing of the saints' feet. Yet some of them have grown up, become pastors, and moved away from the ordinance. Why? Many in the baby boomer generation give the reason that they think feet washing is not "seeker sensitive." The logic goes as follows: If you observe feet washing, then seekers (unchurched people who are visiting your church) will not want to come to a church that does something so strange. In response, pastors with such concerns argue for at least minimizing or diminishing the ritual.

I am afraid to begin doing away with things because they are strange. A lot of people do strange things to get large congregations. Speaking in tongues, for example, is strange, and falling backward and being slain in the spirit is strange. But (non-Free Will Baptist) pastors who use these techniques certainly have no problem drawing crowds and having large megachurches. In fact, it seems that often people in this country are attracted to things that are quizzical and strange.

I don't think it can be shown that doing strange things in church keeps people away. Thus, I don't think we should try so desperately to get away from strange things in church. My wife Melinda grew up in a denomination that practiced infant baptism by sprinkling. Her mother did not believe in the practice. So my wife was not sprinkled until she later became a believer. In fact, I had the privilege of immersing my wife in water baptism. Melinda recalls when she witnessed her first baptism by immersion. My cousin was being baptized at our home church in Pensacola, Florida, and she thought to herself, "How strange. These people have a little mini-swimming-pool back behind the pulpit. They literally have a pool with gallons and gallons of water back of the pulpit."

Baptists are just accustomed to it, but can you imagine being a non-Baptist—let alone an unchurched person—coming to a Baptist church for the first time, and there's a miniature indoor swimming pool? Is it a Jacuzzi? Is it a heated pool? Usually the pool is painted green or blue. It is a strange thing to see in a house of worship! And not only that, but they get this person and dunk him down, holding his nose. He gets up, eyes closed, arms flailing, reaching for a towel.

Let's face it; believer's baptism by immersion is just odd and peculiar. Especially if you are an outsider and you come into this setting, it is most strange. Immersion is now commonplace for my wife, after seeing me baptize many Christian believers, as it becomes for all people who become a part of a Baptist church.

I don't think we want to start doing away with practices because they are perceived by anyone as strange. If one thinks about it, the Lord's Supper is rather strange. The minister says something about breaking bread, but there is no bread, only little bitty white pellets. Everyone is solemn. They pass out these tiny grape juice cups. Why are they so stingy? At least they could have a regular meal with table cloths and at least little Dixie cups with grape juice. This is supposed to be a supper. These people are weird; they're strange! To modern-day Baptists, this is commonplace; it is "no big deal." But think about it; if you were from a totally non-Christian context, both baptism by immersion and the Lord's Supper would seem quite strange.

I come from a Free Will Baptist context in which, when someone was ill and requested it, the pastor would anoint him with oil (James 5:14). How strange this must seem to an outsider! And, of course, the people in my church in Georgia thought it was really strange when I poured oil over their heads, rather than just dabbing my finger in the oil. They thought it was strange until they became accustomed to it.

Strange is a kind of relative term. Many people in the congregation I pastored in South Georgia came from Southern Baptist, Methodist, and other denominational backgrounds. At first, they thought feet washing was strange. But then I preached about the washing of the saints' feet and explained why Free Will Baptists engage in this symbolic ritual. Soon my congregation began to get excited about it, and even the former Baptists and Methodists and those of other denominations who had united with our church became enthusiastic about feet washing. Eventually we were having more people attend the Sunday evenings services in which we observed the Lord's Supper and feet washing than we had on other Sunday evenings. So I think that many times this issue of strangeness is a relative thing.

Many of the people who came to our church had been unchurched people, and those were the people who simply didn't think anything odd at all about washing feet. They were taught this way and surmised that this was the way it was supposed to be. They read John 13, and it was fairly straightforward. So they were not shocked that you would do this in the context of worship. We need to understand that something being strange should not keep us from performing it in church.

EMBARRASSMENT

Growing up, I was not really embarrassed about feet washing. When I got into my college years, I became a little uncomfortable about it. In fact, when I went to Yale University, I was somewhat embarrassed about it, but that's where I lost my embarrassment. Perhaps it was because all these people would ask, "What's the difference between Free Will Baptists and Southern Baptists?" I would say something about Arminianism and the washing of the saints' feet. Then I would almost cringe, waiting for them to laugh, and they would say, "Cool! Washing the saints' feet!" Some of these people did not even believe in the virgin birth. Some did not even believe in the incarnation of Jesus Christ, but they thought that, in a postmodern context, washing of the saints' feet was a meaningful ritual. Soon they wanted to know more about it.

UNCOMFORTABLE

The reason the practice of feet washing has diminished among Free Will Baptists in the last twenty years or so is not because we have submitted it to rigorous biblical, theological, and historical scrutiny and found it wanting. Few Free Will Baptists who have done away with feet washing have studied it in a rigorous way. I think the reason some Free Will Baptists have moved away from feet washing is that they just don't like it. When you pass the plate, get your pellet, get your cup of grape juice, it is not all that uncomfortable. All your Baptist and Presbyterian friends do it. Baptism by immersion is so common among evangelicals that it is not very uncomfortable. But washing feet, much like church discipline, is uncomfortable. We just don't like it.

This reminds me of a conversation I once had with a Free Will Baptist friend of mine who indicated his disapproval of feet washing. I asked him why he was against it, and he said, "Because it's humiliating!" Jeanne Audrey Powers, in an attempt to convince United Methodists to "restore the washing of feet to the church as one of its central rituals" asks the question, "Why does one discern some resistance to the practice?" She then proceeds to ask, "Is it a hesitation to be linked with churches of less social status? Is it that such a ritual, which often produces strong feelings and reactions, smacks of too much emotion in worship?"[14] I think these sorts of considerations

have contributed to the decline of feet washing among Free Will
Baptists in the past few decades.[15]

NOTES

1. R. N. Hinnant, J. C. Griffin, J. O. Fort, and I. J. Blackwelder, eds., *Free Will Baptist Hymnal: Hymns and Gospel Songs for Every Phase of Worship* (Ayden, N.C.: Free Will Baptist Press and Nashville, Tenn.: National Association of Free Will Baptists, 1958), 393.

2. John Shelton Reed, "The Same Old Stand?" in *Why the South Will Survive* (Athens: University of Georgia Press, 1981), 15. Copyright © 1981 by The University of Georgia Press, Athens, Georgia 30602. All rights reserved. Second printing 1983.

3. Paul F. Gillespie, editor of *Foxfire* magazine, asked Elder Ted Nation, Sr., a Free Will Baptist preacher from the mountains of North Carolina, "How do Free Will Baptists feel about snake handling?" Elder Nation's reply was like that of other Free Will Baptists, simply: "I'd handle a snake all right if his head was cut off and I had on gloves." Paul F. Gillespie, ed., *Foxfire 7* (Garden City: Anchor/Doubleday, 1982), 83.

4. See Howard Dorgan, *Giving Glory to God in Appalachia: Worship Practices of Six Baptist Subdenominations* (Knoxville: University of Tennessee Press, 1987) Used with permission.

5. This includes both Pentecostal (Cleveland, Tennessee) and non-Pentecostal (Anderson, Indiana, and General Conference).

6. This is the denomination with which Grace Theological Seminary in Winona Lake, Indiana, is affiliated.

7. While not viewing it as one of their seven sacraments, Roman Catholics have for centuries observed feet washing, especially on "Maundy Thursday." (This is similar to the practice of the Eastern Orthodox churches.) Catholics consider feet washing as a "sacramental," i.e., something slightly less efficacious than a full-fledged sacrament. John A. Hardon *The Catholic Catechism: A Contemporary Catechism of the Teachings of the Catholic Church* (Garden City: Doubleday, 1975), 548-49. Cf. D. H. Stamatis, *A Catechetical Handbook of the Eastern Orthodox Church* (Minneapolis: Light and Life, 2003), 280-81; Philip Schaff, *A History of the Christian Church* (Grand Rapids: Eerdmans, [1910], 1950), 3:402.

8. Philip Schaff, *A History of the Christian Church* (Grand Rapids: Eerdmans, [1907] 1952), 5:355. This volume is authored by David Schaff.

9. William Jeffrey, *The Whole Faith of Man: Being the Gospel Declared in Plainness, as It Is in Jesus* (London: Francis Smith, 1659), 102. A precursor to the *1812 Abstract*, Jeffrey's work also affirms baptism, the Lord's Supper, laying on of hands, anointing the sick with oil, and prayer with fasting as ordinances.

10. *An Abstract of the Former Articles of Faith Confessed by the Original Baptist Church Holding the Doctrine of General Provision. With a Proper Code of Discipline for the Future Government of the Church,* Newbern, N.C.: (Salmon Hall, 1813, authorized 1812), Article XVII. This confession of faith is reprinted in J. Matthew Pinson, *A Free Will Baptist Handbook: Heritage, Beliefs, and Ministries* (Nashville: Randall House, 1998), 142-47.

11. *A Treatise of the Faith and Practices of the National Association of Free Will Baptists,* Nashville: Executive Office, National Association of Free Will Baptists, rev. 1996, "The Faith of Free Will Baptists," chapter XIII. Hereinafter referred to as *Treatise.*

12. *Treatise,* "Articles of Faith," Article 13.

13. *Treatise,* "The Practices of Free Will Baptists," chapter 1, section 6.

14. Jeanne Audrey Powers, *Ritual in a New Day: An Invitation* [a study of the Alternate Rituals Project of the Section on Worship of the Board of Discipleship of the United Methodist Church] (Nashville: Discipleship Resources, 1976), 25, 27. Out of print.

15. Occasionally one will hear someone who objects to feet washing on the grounds of hygiene (the use of a common basin). For this reason, as well as efficiency, some groups, like the Grace Brethren youth convention, have begun using individual moist towelettes. Some people suggest that the reason more Free Will Baptists do not observe feet washing is that congregations are often dismissed after the Lord's Supper. Many ministers who have begun pastoring such churches have found that making reverent transitional statements and reading relevant Scripture passages after the Lord's Supper, rather than simply dismissing the congregation, results in greater attendance at the washing of the saints' feet.

LOVE CONSECRATES THE HUMBLEST ACT

May be sung in unison

1. Love con-se-crates the hum-blest act, And sanc-ti-fies each deed.
2. "Ye call Me Lord and Mas-ter, all, Yet I would hum-bly bow

It sheds a ben-e-dict-ion sweet, And hal-lows ev-'ry need.
And con-se-crate this low-ly deed, As ye be-hold Me now.

When in the shad-ow of the cross, Christ bowed and washed the feet
As I have done this un-to you, My breth-ren, here this night,
3. Love serves, yet will-ing stoops to serve, What Christ in love so true

2nd time D.S.

Of His dis-ci-ples, 'twas a sign Of His great love com-plete.
Thus would I have you do to each When I have passed from sight."
Hath free-ly done for one and all, Shall we not glad-ly do?

S. B. McManus, 1902
8.6.8.6.D (3rd stanza 8.6.8.6.)

Southern Harmony, 1835
Arr. © 2006 by James M. Stevens
RESIGNATION

WHAT IS AN ORDINANCE?

Chapter Two

CHAPTER TWO

Why do we believe that the washing of the saints' feet is an ordinance? First we must define the word *ordinance*. Interestingly, there is no definition of that word in the New Testament. The way we have tended to use it in the Protestant world does not even seem to be the way the New Testament uses it. So I will briefly discuss the history of the concept of ordinances or what Presbyterians, Lutherans, Episcopalians, and Catholics, for example, call sacraments. We tend to use the word *ordinance* to speak of these things; those traditions use the word *sacrament*.

THE HISTORICAL BACKGROUND OF SACRAMENTS

The church fathers in early Christianity did not define, enumerate, or classify sacraments or ordinances. They did not have a well-worked-out sacramental theology. In fact, the concept of sacraments did not take shape until the end of the seventh century. Yet Augustine of Hippo (354-430) had set into motion the central medieval Catholic notion of the sacraments: that sacraments convey divine grace.

The view that the sacraments transmit divine grace contributed to the theological context of the Protestant Reformation. The *Thirty-Nine Articles* of the Reformation Church of England exemplify the Magisterial Protestant view of the sacraments.[1] They are very direct about the nature of sacraments as conveyors of grace: "Sacraments ordained of Christ be not only badges or tokens of Christian men's profession, but rather they be certain sure witnesses, and effectual signs of grace, and God's good will toward us, by the which he doth work invisibly in us, and doth not only quicken, but also strengthen and confirm our Faith in him."[2] Martin Luther made his views clear in such statements as the following from his *Short Catechism* (1529):

> What is the Sacrament of the Altar? *Answer.* It is the very Body and Blood of our Lord Jesus Christ, under the Bread and Wine, for us Christians to eat and to drink. What avails us to eat and drink thus? *Answer.* This is shown us by the words which stand there, *"Given for you and shed for you for the remission of sins."* That is to say, that in the Sacrament forgiveness of sins, life, and salvation are bestowed on us by these words.[3]

With the exception of the Anabaptists and Baptists, most early Protestants—Lutheran, Reformed, and Anglican—believed that the sacraments in some way conveyed divine grace.

This understanding of sacraments predisposed the Magisterial Reformers to adopt baptism and the Lord's Supper as the two sacraments that most logically convey divine grace. So they did away with the other five of the seven medieval Roman Catholic sacraments and held onto baptism and the Lord's Supper.

THE HISTORICAL BACKGROUND OF ORDINANCES

The Anabaptists—the forefathers of what we know as Mennonites, the Church of the Brethren, Hutterians, and Amish—wholly rejected sacramentalism. The early Anabaptists influenced our own English General Baptist forefathers, John Smyth and Thomas Helwys, when they were exiled from England to Amsterdam and came into contact with the Dutch Waterlander Mennonites.

The Anabaptists rejected sacramentalism and wanted to go back and recapture the essence of New Testament Christianity. In their view, the ordinances, far from conveying divine grace, were *symbols* or *pictures* that *memorialize* Christ and His gospel. The Anabaptists simply affirmed that ordinances are sacred rites ordained by God. That was their definition. Thus, they freed themselves from any preconceived notion of sacraments, whether Catholic or Protestant, whether seven or two. The number of ordinances therefore varied from one Anabaptist to another. For example, Dirk Phillips, a prominent sixteenth-century Anabaptist, taught seven Christian ordinances, one of which was "the foot washing of the saints."[4] The General Baptists, our forefathers in England, also maintained a much more open-ended definition of the ordinances, much like the Anabaptists. In this way, they differed from their Particular Baptist brothers and sisters.

The Particular Baptists, the strong Calvinists of the seventeenth-century English Baptist movement, adopted the Westminster Confession of Faith approach to the ordinances, but they substituted the word *ordinance* for *sacrament*.[5] They had a much more Magisterial Reformation-oriented view of the ordinances. They believed that something happens graciously when we partake of the ordinances—that they are not a mere picture or symbol of a special grace but are actually special grace taking place in some way.[6]

THE ARBITRARINESS OF DEFINITIONS

Anabaptist and General Baptist approaches to the ordinances tended to hold that typical Catholic and Protestant definitions of sacraments or ordinances were arbitrary because they could not be found in Holy Scripture. According to this view, the detailed Catholic and Protestant definitions of sacraments are extra-biblical in nature. One cannot determine the definition of the words *ordinance* and *sacrament* from the New Testament. The New Testament does not speak in these terms. So, for example, the common view that a sacrament or an ordinance is a sign or a symbol that is ordained by Christ to be perpetuated in the church and that it must "typify Christ" is simply not to be found in the New Testament.[7] As much as we might believe that feet washing conforms to this definition, it is still an extra-biblical definition. And the Anabaptist and Baptist traditions came closer to understanding this. They understood that the whole medieval sacramental system and that of the Protestant Reformation was a human creation. One could not extrapolate from Holy Scripture the definition of an ordinance. An ordinance is simply something God has *ordained*.

This reminds me of the first time I asked Leroy Forlines to define the term *ordinance*. He responded, "It depends on whom you're talking to. Basically, most people decide on which practices are ordinances and then make a definition that fits." And really that is true. Baptists, for example, typically give a definition that is tailor-made for baptism and the Lord's Supper. Presbyterians, Lutherans, and Episcopalians go back to creedal and confessional definitions. However, most Baptists simply say that an ordinance is what baptism and the Lord's Supper are, and they attempt to define it as strictly as possible so that nothing else can be considered an ordinance. That is what Mr. Forlines told me. This, of course, was not the answer that I had hoped for.[8]

EXTRA-BIBLICAL DEFINITIONS

The concept of ordinances as conceived today is simply not a biblical construct. This truth clears the decks. After years of thinking about Mr. Forlines's response, it finally occurred to me that any attempt to limit the number of ordinances by criteria other than *being ordained by God in the New Testament* is not a biblical endeavor.

I recently had a discussion with a Free Will Baptist pastor who asked me, "Why do we have three ordinances instead of two? Why have we added this third ordinance—feet washing?" Other Baptists often ask us this question. I answered him by saying, "That is not a biblical question." What I meant is that this question, why three ordinances instead of two, is not a question that the New Testament leads us to ask. We ask it because we feel the need to use non-biblical criteria that we have unconsciously derived from the Protestant tradition to justify our definition of ordinances. Yet the question arises out of an interaction with Protestant theology, not out of an interaction with the New Testament. The question Scripture compels us to ask regarding the ordinances may not be why we have three ordinances instead of two. It might be why we have three ordinances instead of six, eight, or eleven. In other words, it is better simply to say that ordinances are just things God ordains in the New Covenant Scriptures.

That is the definition of the *1812 Abstract*, that early Free Will Baptist confession I quoted in chapter one:

> We believe, as touching gospel ordinances, in believers'
> baptism, laying on of hands, receiving the sacrament[9] in
> bread and wine, washing the saints' feet, anointing the

sick with oil in the name of the Lord, fasting, prayer, singing praise to God, and the public ministry of the Word, *with every institution of the Lord we shall find in the New Testament* (Mark 15:15,16; Acts 8:17; 19:6; Luke 22:19, 20; John 13:5-17; James 5:14).[10]

The bottom line is that, if the New Testament says to do it, we are going to do it. If God *ordains* it, it is an *ordinance* for us, and we will fulfill it. So my suggestion is that one must go to Scripture inductively to ascertain what an ordinance is. One must avoid going to the Bible deductively, with a preconceived notion of ordinances based on medieval or modern criteria. Perhaps the best thing to do is begin qualifying the word *ordinance*. Maybe that is what is so confusing for people. Perhaps we should simply say we are doing what Jesus said to do in the church. If indeed feet washing is a ritual that Jesus perpetuated for use in the church, it matters not what one calls it; the church needs to do it.

The Bible has an open-ended definition of ordinances—*any ritual or non-ritual act that God ordains for perpetuation by His people,* the *ekklesia,* the assembly of God, the church. Yet even by the standard Baptist definition of ordinance, the washing of the saints' feet measures up. It fits even by the most delimiting, exacting definition.

STANDARD BAPTIST DEFINITIONS OF ORDINANCES

Let's look at some definitions of "ordinance" that Baptists have proposed:

A. H. Strong: "those outward rites which Christ has appointed to be administered in his church as visible signs of the saving truth of the gospel. They are signs, in that they vividly express this truth and confirm it in the believer."[11]

W. T. Conner: "pictorial representations of the fundamental facts of the gospel and of our salvation through the gospel . . . instituted by Christ, for a very obvious reason. That reason is that they are adapted to set forth the facts of the gospel and our experience of salvation through grace."[12]

Henry G. Weston: "an outward institution, appointed by Christ, by positive precept, to be observed by all his people to the end of the age, commemorating an essential fact and declaring an essential gospel truth."[13]

Alvah Hovey: "emblematic of central facts in the Christian religion; and together [the ordinances] teach in a very impressive manner the vital doctrines of the gospel."[14]

From these definitions we can construct a standard Baptist view of the basic elements of an ordinance: (1) It must be an outward ritual. (2) It must be ordained by Christ to be (3) literally perpetuated by His people. (4) It must be pictorially symbolic. As to *what* a ritual must pictorially symbolize to be an ordinance, these authors do not agree. Weston indicates that an ordinance must symbolize an "essential gospel truth"; Strong, "the saving truth of the gospel"; Hovey, "the vital doctrines of the gospel." Conner's definition is a bit more open-ended. He argues that an ordinance is symbolic of "the facts of the gospel and our experience of salvation through grace." W. A. Criswell decides to best them all, offering a definition that is a stereotype of the method Forlines spoke of—choosing which rituals you want to be ordinances and then defining accordingly. Criswell says that for a ritual to be an ordinance, it must be "a picture of the atonement of the Lord Jesus Christ."[15] So, by saying that an ordinance must symbolize

Christ's atonement and only Christ's atonement, one constructs an edifice around the doctrine of "the two ordinances" that seems impregnable. Yet such an edifice rests on a sandy foundation because the definition is arbitrary.

PROBLEMS WITH THE ABOVE DEFINITIONS

What are we to make of these standard Baptist definitions of "ordinance"? Before answering that question, I will offer a composite definition that seeks to do justice to all the above definitions, including Criswell's:

> An ordinance is an outward ritual that Christ ordained for perpetuation by His New Covenant People, pictorially to symbolize for and to confirm in them the redemptive significance of His life and death.

If this is an accurate composite (and I think it is), should we not accept this as a valid definition of *ordinance*? Feet washing fits all these criteria. Yet this is an invalid definition of ordinances because it is entirely arbitrary. One searches in vain for any scriptural warrant for these definitions. Who told these men that this was the definition of an ordinance? Where, for example, did Criswell read in Holy Scripture that "an ordinance must symbolize the atonement of the Lord Jesus Christ"? For that matter, how did we find out that something can be an ordinance only if it were ordained by *Christ*? Are the Father and Holy Spirit any less God than Christ? If, for instance, the Holy Spirit, through the apostle James, ordained the anointing of the sick with oil in the name of the Lord, is this any less an ordinance because the Holy Spirit ordained it rather than Christ?

How should we respond to such a definition? Elements of these Baptist definitions of ordinances are correct and viable. Yet we must admit that their most important elements are arbitrary and lack scriptural warrant. Having said that, I must add that we can use these definitions to show that *feet washing must be considered an ordinance even by the most exacting of these arbitrary standards.*

SCRIPTURAL CRITERIA FOR ORDINANCES

We need to avoid creating arbitrary definitions for ordinances. So, what are the appropriate questions to ask to establish if something is an ordinance? The first question must obviously be, did God explicitly ordain the practice? Of course, if Christ ordained a given practice, we can answer the question in the affirmative. No biblical scholar of any tradition would deny that Christ ordained feet washing in John 13. On the next question, the primary objection to feet washing as an ordinance arises: Did God intend the practice to be *literal*? This will be discussed in chapter three. A third important question is: Is it to be perpetuated by God's people? Asking these three questions deals with some but not all of the components of the composite Baptist definition above. We have insisted that we must not be constrained to say that, to be considered an ordinance, a practice must have been ordained by Christ only and not by one of the other two persons of the Holy Trinity. This is completely arbitrary.

Now we are left with the following questions: What about the ritual status of an ordinance? and What about the symbolism of an ordinance? Again, we must understand that these are arbitrary questions that Scripture does not compel us to ask, though the washing of the saints' feet answers both these questions satisfactorily.

First, some things ordained by God may or may not be ritual in nature. Practices like prayer, worship, and the public ministry of the word are not ritual in nature. Things like baptism, laying on of hands, the Lord's Supper, feet washing, and anointing the sick with oil are rituals. Any definition of *ordinance* that stipulates that non-ritual ordinances are not Christian ordinances is derived from some other source than Holy Scripture.

Second, the Baptist definitions above insisted that, to be an ordinance, a practice must be a symbol of the redemptive significance of the life and death of Christ for us. We must again admit that some things ordained by God in Scripture do not so readily conform to this demand. Anointing the sick with oil, for instance, is not explicitly and directly symbolic of the redemptive significance of Christ's life and death for us, though it is symbolic of related gospel truths.

The definition of an ordinance we are left with is as follows: *A Christian ordinance is a practice that God ordained for literal perpetuation by the New Covenant People of God.*

NOTES

1. "Magisterial Reformers" refers to the "mainline" Reformers in the Protestant Reformation who had the backing of the secular government. This is used in distinction to the Radical Reformers or Anabaptists who did not believe the church should be controlled by the state or *vice versa*.

2. From "Articles of Religion," article 25, in *The Book of Common Prayer* (New York: James Pott and Company, 1892), 652.

3. Martin Luther, "The Short Catechism, 1529," in Henry Bettenson, ed., *Documents of the Christian Church* (New York: Oxford University Press, 1947), 293-94.

4. Timothy George, *Theology of the Reformers* (Nashville: Broadman, 1988), 294. Used by permission.

5. The Particular Baptist "Second London Confession" was essentially the Presbyterian-inspired "Westminster Confession of Faith" shorn of infant baptism and presbyterial ecclesiology. See "The Assembly or Second London Confession, 1677 and 1688," in William L. Lumpkin, ed., *Baptist Confessions of Faith* (Valley Forge, Pa.: Judson, 1969), 235-95.

6. For more reflections on the historical background of sacraments and ordinances, see the appendix to this book, "Historical Reflections on Ordinances and Sacraments."

7. This is from the early Southern Baptist theologian John Leadley Dagg, who said, "It is an argument of weight against regarding the washing of feet as a religious ceremony instituted in the church, that it does not, like baptism and the Lord's Supper, *typify* Christ," *A Treatise of Church Order*, originally published in 1858. Repr. Harrisonburg, Va.: Gano, 1990, 229. *Contra* Dagg, the argument of this book is twofold: (1) Even though the New Testament does not define ordinances in this way, (2) feet washing does indeed typify Christ like baptism and the Lord's Supper. This will be discussed primarily in chapters four and six.

8. This is similar to the time I asked him on the way to a theological meeting, "Why is it that most Free Will Baptist say 'feet washing' and not 'foot washing.'" His answer—again, not what I expected—was, "Because there are two." It made sense to me.

9. The term *sacrament* here is used not in a technical but in a popular sense.

10. *An Abstract of the Former Articles of Faith Confessed by the Original Baptist Church Holding the Doctrine of General Provision. With a Proper Code of Discipline for the Future Government of the Church* (Newbern, N.C.: Salmon Hall, 1813, authorized 1812), Article XVII. This confession of faith is reprinted in J. Matthew Pinson, *A Free Will Baptist Handbook: Heritage, Beliefs, and Ministries* (Nashville: Randall House, 1998), 142-47. (Italics added.)

11. Augustus Hopkins Strong, *Systematic Theology* (Philadelphia: Judson, 1907), 930.

12. W. T. Conner, *Christian Doctrine* (Nashville: Broadman, 1937), 273. Used by permission.

13. E. H. Johnson and Henry G. Weston, *An Outline of Systematic Theology and of Ecclesiology* (Philadelphia: American Baptist Publication Society, 1895), 329.

14. Alvah Hovey, *Manual of Systematic Theology and Christian Ethics* (Philadelphia: American Baptist Publication Society, 1877), 312.

15. W. A. Criswell, *The Doctrine of the Church* (Nashville: Convention, 1980), 82. Used by permission.

THE BASIN AND THE TOWEL

1. That Thou, Cre - a - tion's Lord, didst think
2. That Thou, the God of Earth and Heaven
3. Grant us, O Christ, the mind pos - sessed,
4. The ba - sin and the towel we take

To count the place of ser - vice meet!
Shouldst gird Thee with our low - ly frame!
When Thou didst reck - on self for naught;
As em - blems of our self dis - dain;

That, in Thy beau - ty, didst not shrink
That, in Thy pure - ness, shouldst be given
When Thou wast cursed that we be blessed,
We glad - ly our own good for - sake,

To wash the wretch - ed crea - ture's feet!
To drink the cup of hu - man blame!
When Thou wast spent that we be bought.
And seek, hence - forth, our broth - er's gain.

Robert Picirilli
© 1963 Robert Picirilli
L.M.

Arr. from *Katholisches Gesangbuch*, Vienna, c. 1774
HURSLEY

APPOINTED BY CHRIST
FOR LITERAL PERPETUATION

Chapter Three

CHAPTER THREE

And supper being ended, the devil having already put it into the heart of Judas Iscariot, Simon's son, to betray Him, Jesus, knowing that the Father had given all things into His hands, and that He had come from God and was going to God, rose from supper and laid aside His garments, took a towel and girded Himself. After that, He poured water into a basin and began to wash the disciples' feet, and to wipe them with the towel with which He was girded. Then He came to Simon Peter. And Peter said to Him, "Lord, are You washing my feet?"

Jesus answered and said to him, "What I am doing you do not understand now, but you will know after this."

Peter said to Him, "You shall never wash my feet!"

Jesus answered him, "If I do not wash you, you have no part with Me."

Simon Peter said to Him, "Lord, not my feet only, but also my hands and my head!"

Jesus said to him, "He who is bathed needs only to wash his feet, but is completely clean; and you are clean, but not all of you." For He knew who would betray Him; therefore He said, "You are not all clean."

So when He had washed their feet, taken His garments, and sat down again, He said to them, "Do you know what I have done to you? You call Me Teacher and Lord, and you say well, for so I am. If I then, your Lord and Teacher, have washed your feet, you also ought to wash one another's feet. For I have given you an example, that you should do as I have done to you. Most assuredly, I say to you, a servant is not greater than his master, nor is he who is sent greater than he who sent him. If you know these things, blessed are you if you do them.

—John 13:2-17

In the last chapter, we discussed Baptist definitions of *ordinance* and how they were arbitrary, that is, not based on Scripture. A. H. Strong's definition is representative. It may be summarized as follows: Outward rites Christ has appointed to be administered in His church, visible signs of the saving truth of the gospel that express it and confirm it in the believer. As I said in the last chapter, I don't believe that this definition is necessary for a church practice to be an ordinance. However, let's play ball in our opponent's court and see how feet washing measures up to this arbitrary, non-scriptural definition of ordinance.

RITUAL SYMBOL

First of all, let us consider the washing of feet as a *visible sign*. This means that the washing of the saints' feet in John 13 was symbolic ritual. It was *not*, as some of the older Baptist theologians said, a mere civic or civil custom.[1] If we are to understand the washing of the saints' feet as a *ritual* that the churches should practice liturgically (in their worship), then we must demonstrate that Jesus was not washing the disciples' feet just to get them clean! He was engaging in symbolic ritual, not ordinary custom.[2] It wasn't Jesus just washing their feet to get them clean because they hadn't washed their feet yet. That was a common practice in that day because people wore sandals, and they got their feet dirty on dusty streets. There would be a basin and a servant or slave to wash the traveler's feet. So the question is, was Jesus just doing that?

The first thing to consider about that assertion is that few contemporary biblical interpreters say that Jesus was washing the disciples' feet merely to get the dust off. Had this been so, why would Jesus have made such a big deal out of it?[3] Jesus rises after supper has already been served and begins this very ceremonial act of taking off His cloak, laying it to the side, and kneeling to wash the disciples' feet. Why was Jesus going to such great lengths on this occasion if He were just observing a customary, ordinary practice? A cursory reading of John 13 demonstrates that He was using ritual symbol to teach the disciples. This refutes the objection against feet washing raised by some writers in the nineteenth century that the washing of the disciples' feet was a mere act of civility.

APPOINTED BY CHRIST

The next thing that Strong says is that an ordinance must have been *appointed by Christ* to be administered in His church. The first thing I see from John 13, and the thing Free Will Baptists have said for centuries, is simply this: Jesus says you *ought* to do it (verses 14, 15). Robert Picirilli, in the *Randall House Bible Commentary* on the gospel of John, explains that "ought" means that one is *bound* or *obligated* to do something.[4] Jesus says you ought to do this. He is saying to the disciples, "Look at what I've done to you. You are *bound* and *obligated* to do this to each other." When He says that, we have to accept it. We have to sit up and take notice and say to ourselves, what is He talking about here? Does He mean that this should be a literal practice, or is He just saying you need to be humble to people?

THE WORDS OF INSTITUTION

Traditionally, analysis of Jesus' *words of institution* has played a central role in establishing whether something He commanded constitutes a sacrament or ordinance. When we compare John 13 with the passages where Jesus mentions baptism and the Lord's Supper, we discover that the words of institution for feet washing are *much stronger* than the words of institution for baptism or the Lord's Supper.[5] Let's look at baptism. Below are all of Jesus' commands regarding baptism.

> "Make disciples of all the nations, baptizing them . . . " (Matthew 28:19, 20).

> "He who believes and is baptized will be saved . . ." (Mark 16:16).

That is the extent of Jesus' commands regarding baptism. His commands regarding the Lord's Supper are all recorded by the synoptic gospel writers from the same event. Jesus says only *one* thing regarding the Lord's Supper, and the three synoptic writers record it.

> "Take, eat; this is My body. . . . Drink from it, all of you" (Matthew 26:26, 27).

> "Take, eat; this is My body. . . . This is My blood of the new covenant . . . " (Mark 14:22, 23).

> "This is My body which is given for you; do this in remembrance of Me. . . . This cup is the new covenant in My blood, which is shed for you" (Luke 22:19, 20).

Now listen to Jesus' statements regarding the feet washing.

> "What I am doing you do not understand now, but you will know after this" (John 13:7).

> "Do you know what I have done to you?" (John 13:12).

> "If I then, your Lord and teacher, have washed your feet, you also ought to wash one another's feet" (John 13:14).

> "For I have given you an example, that you should do as I have done to you" (John 13:15).

> "If you know these things, blessed are you if you do them" (John 13:17).

The question whether Jesus Christ instituted the washing of feet for perpetuation in His church should be answered by this look at the text. Jesus mentioned baptism at most twice, and He mentioned the Lord's Supper once in just a few words in the synoptic Gospels.

When one looks at the amount of "red letters" in the narratives of Jesus about the institution of baptism and the Lord's Supper, and then at the amount of red letters in the institution of the washing of the saints' feet, the difference is remarkable. Jesus goes on for fourteen verses—going into great detail about washing feet, discussing with Peter about it, explaining the significance of it much more than He explained that of baptism or the Lord's Supper.

A LITERAL RITUAL PRACTICE

Whether or not Jesus *instituted* feet washing seems to be fairly settled. The question that remains is, did Jesus intend the practice to be *literal?* I don't think anyone these days is going to say that Jesus did not institute the washing of the saints' feet to be observed by His church. Those who object to the ritual washing of feet would simply say, rather, that in instituting the washing of the saints' feet, what Jesus was really saying is, "You need to do humble things for people." So we must ask the question, is the practice intended to be literal, and the answer is yes.[6]

QUAKERS AND THE LITERALNESS OF ORDINANCES

It is interesting that, historically, Quakers have believed that *all* these ordinances are sensual and fleshly and the church should not observe them. None of them is to be observed literally—not baptism, the Lord's Supper, feet washing, or anointing with oil. All of those practices, they have argued, have passed away; they are fleshly and sensual. We, as the New Covenant church, are *spiritual*, they have said; all has been made new. Thus, Quakers have traditionally argued that Protestants and Catholics err in taking these commands literally.

Robert Barclay, a famous Quaker in seventeenth-century England, said in his *Apology for the True Christian Divinity*, "If we look into the plain scripture, what can be thence inferred to urge the one [the Lord's Supper], which may not be likewise pleaded for the other [the washing of the saints' feet]?"[7] Barclay did not believe in the observance of either the Lord's Supper or feet washing. He was trying to say to the Presbyterians and Baptists, who were arguing that the Lord's Supper and baptism were really ordinances, your arguments against washing feet can just as easily be turned on your arguments for the Lord's Supper and baptism. So he asks,

> What can be thence inferred to urge the one [the Lord's Supper], which may not be likewise pleaded for the other [feet washing]; or for laying aside the one [feet washing], which may not be likewise said against the continuance of the other [the Lord's Supper]? If they say, *That the former, of washing the feet, was only a ceremony;* what have they, whence they can show, that this *breaking of bread* is more? If they say, *That the former was only a sign of humility and purifying;* what have they to prove that this was more? If they say, *That one was only for a time, and was no evangelical ordinance;* what hath this to make it such, that the other wanted? Surely there is no way of reason to evade this; neither can any thing be alleged, that the one should cease, and not the other; or the one continue, and not the other. . . . But

since the former, to wit, *the washing of one another's feet,* is justly laid aside, as not binding upon *Christians;* so ought also the other for the same reason.[8]

Free Will Baptists would agree with Barclay that there is no reason to accept the Lord's Supper if one doesn't accept feet washing.

LITERAL OR FIGURATIVE?

The main objection to the washing of the saints' feet is that Jesus did not intend Christians to practice it literally, but only figuratively in daily acts of humility.[9] This idea arises from the fact that non-feet-washers cannot seem to get away from the idea that feet washing symbolizes *only* humility.[10] Only recently have biblical scholars begun to recognize the broad symbolism in John 13. They have begun to realize that Christ was not only commanding humility, but He was also symbolizing the redemptive significance of His life and death and the radical transformation of the one who experiences union with Him. [11]

Thus people who have argued against feet washing as an ordinance have relied on the assumption that Jesus was commanding only daily acts of humility. They say that the church does not need a ritual that reminds believers of humility; Christians do this simply in daily, humble acts. The reason most non-feet-washers do not observe feet washing as an ordinance is not because they do not think it should be *perpetuated* in the church, but because they do not believe Jesus commanded its *literal* practice in the church. So the issue is not whether the washing of feet should be perpetuated—no one will say that humble acts should not be perpetuated. The issue is whether it is a command for *literal* reenactment or merely humble acts.

Non-feet-washers would be harder pressed to argue against feet washing as a literal practice if they understood that it symbolizes more than just humility. The problem is that people who observe the washing of the saints' feet have done so little research and scholarship to demonstrate to non-feet-washers that this is the case. If humility were the only thing the washing of the saints' feet pictures, it would be easier to think Jesus was only commanding acts of humility. However, that position becomes more difficult to maintain when one realizes that feet washing symbolizes the incarnation and sanctification (this will be discussed in chapter four). If non-feet-washers were brought to an understanding of the incarnational and sanctificational imagery in feet washing, how could they insist that Jesus did not command its literal practice?

In other words, it is one thing to say:

In John 13 Jesus is just telling us to be humble.

It is another thing to say:

[A] In John 13 Jesus is just telling us to symbolize the incarnation in our everyday lives.

Saying that Jesus is just telling us to symbolize the incarnation in our everyday lives would be ludicrous, since Jesus just happened to give us a ritual with which to symbolize the incarnation. This second statement would be like saying:

[B] When Jesus says to eat bread and drink wine in remembrance of Himself, He is really just saying to celebrate His death in our everyday lives.

What's the formal difference between these sayings [A] and [B] above? There is none.

That's the Quaker argument. That's what they say to all of us: When Jesus says to eat bread and drink wine in remembrance of Himself, He is really just saying to celebrate His death in our everyday lives. They argue that the Lord's Supper is merely a command to *die daily* and be crucified with Christ. They contend that Christ did not require its *literal* perpetuation.

If one believes that Christ commanded the literal practice of the Lord's Supper because of its symbolism of His death, one is logically compelled to believe that Christ commanded the literal practice of feet washing because of its symbolism of His incarnation and of sanctification. If one acknowledges that Jesus in the upper room performed two ritual acts, and they both symbolize central truths about His life and death, then something *external* must enter into one's reasoning to show that one ritual must be practiced literally and the other must not.

Those who practice feet washing simply point to both Gospel accounts and say that the words of institution for feet washing are as strong as, if not stronger than, those for the Lord's Supper. The language itself—what Jesus said with regard to the two practices—is not significantly different between the Lord's Supper account and the feet washing account. Furthermore, the concepts of incarnation, sanctification, and love and humble service (feet washing) are no less suited to being symbolized in a literal ritual practice than Christ's death is (Lord's Supper). In other words, Christ gave one symbol (bread and wine) to symbolize His death and another symbol (basin and towel) to symbolize His humility and incarnation and our sanctification, and He used very similar words to command observance of both rituals:

"this do" for the Lord's Supper and "you ought [are obligated] to do" for feet washing.

Those who argue that feet washing is not a literal church practice but just a first-century object lesson must show why the Lord's Supper is not just an object lesson, as the Quakers argue. However, one must go outside of the Gospels to establish that the Lord's Supper is a literal ritual practice and feet washing is merely a first-century object lesson. That brings us to the subject of the next chapter.

NOTES

1. As Leon Morris comments, "It was an action undertaken deliberately, and not simply the usual act of courtesy" (*The Gospel of John* in the *New International Commentary on the New Testament* [Grand Rapids: Eerdmans, 1995], 544).

2. My use of *ritual* is similar to David R. Plaster's word *ceremony*. Plaster says that feet washing, like baptism and the Lord's Supper, is a "physical act which is ceremonial in nature. What does the word 'ceremonial' mean? By its simple definition a ceremony is understood to be 'a formal act or series of acts prescribed by ritual, protocol, or convention' or 'prescribed procedures'" (*Ordinances: What Are They?* [Winona Lake, Ind.: BMH, 1985], 33). Allen Edgington, like Plaster a Grace Brethren scholar, asks: "Can it be concluded that the action of Jesus was ceremonial in nature? As I have shown above, Jesus was not simply carrying out a usual procedure. The significance was greater than the physical act. Neither was the application of truth to a ceremonial act something new to the disciples. God had already done so with the washing of the hands and feet of the Israelite priests (Exodus 30:17–21; 40:30–32)—this act too was ceremonial in nature" ("Footwashing as an Ordinance," *Grace Theological Journal* 6/2 [1985], 426-35, 428).

3. The seventeenth-century Quaker Robert Barclay wondered why so many Protestants rejected feet washing while embracing baptism and the Lord's Supper, given the fact that the description of feet washing is so much more vivid than that of the other two: "If we regard the narration of this [the feet washing account in John 13], and the circumstances attending it, it was done with far more solemnity, and prescribed far more punctually and particularly than the former. It is said only, *As he was eating, he took bread;* so that this would seem to be but an *occasional business:* but here *he rose up, he laid by his garments, he girded himself, he poured out the water, he washed their feet, he wiped them with a towel:* he did this to all of them; which are circumstances surely far more observable than those noted in the other. . . . In the former he saith, as it were

passingly, *Do this in remembrance of me;* but here he sitteth down again, he desires them to consider what he hath done, tells them positively, *that as he hath done to them, so ought they to do to one another:* and yet again he redoubles that precept, by telling them, *he has given them an example, that they should do so likewise.* . . . I would willingly propose this seriously to men, who will be pleased to make use of that reason and understanding that God hath given them, and not be imposed upon, nor abused by the custom or tradition of others; *Whether this ceremony, if we respect either the time that it was appointed in, or the circumstances where with it was performed, or the command enjoining the use of it, hath not as much to recommend it for a standing ordinance of the gospel, as either water-baptism, or bread and wine, or any other of that kind?"* (Robert Barclay, *An Apology for the True Christian Divinity: Being an Explanation and Vindication of the Principles and Doctrines of the People Called Quakers,* 8th ed. [New York: Samuel Wood and Sons, 1827].

4. Jack W. Stallings, *John* in the *Randall House Bible Commentary* (Nashville: Randall House, 1989), 192. F. Hauck comments that the word *ought* signifies "an obligation towards men which is deduced and which follows from the experienced or preceding act of God the Savior. In many instances the sentence construction indicates the connection between human obligation and the experienced act of salvation." G. Kittel and G. Friedrich, eds., *Theological Dictionary of the New Testament* (trans. G. W. Bromiley; 10 vols; Grand Rapids: Eerdmans, 1964-74), 5:563.

5. John Christopher Thomas argues that the original readers of John's gospel would know that the foot washing took place in the context of the Last Supper. This context, he says, "would raise the readers' expectations in regard to words of institution. In other words, the 'eucharistic' setting would prepare the readers for the institution of a sacred rite. Read against this backdrop, vv. 14-17 sound very much like words of institution." John Christopher Thomas, *Footwashing in John 13 and the Johannine Community* (Sheffield, England: University of Sheffield Academic Press, 1991), 128.

6. John Christopher Thomas remarks that "the narrative contains not one, but three directives to the disciples to practice footwashing. It seems improbable that either the disciples (in the narrative) or the implied readers would understand such emphatic language as not having as its primary reference the actual practice of footwashing." In another place he argues that "the implied readers would understand vv. 14-17 in a literal fashion. This assessment is due in large part to the straightforward character of the language. After all, the text does indeed contain explicit commands for the disciples to wash one another's feet. These commands are not inferences in these verses but the clear wording of the text. . . . In addition, when the commands of 13.14-17 are read against the cultural context of Western antiquity, it seems even more probable that the first readers . . . would have taken vv. 14-17 as calling for literal compliance on their part." (Thomas, 112; 127, 28.) Similarly, Craig Keener says: "Did the Johannine community practice, or did the Johannine Jesus expect them to practice, literal foot washing to represent his teachings about serving one another? . . . It is very likely that John would approve, and even possible that he did intend, his audience to practice such a symbol. Greeks and Romans practiced ritual foot washing, and foot washing appears in cultic settings in early Jewish sources." (*The Gospel of John: A Commentary* [Peabody, Mass.: Hendrickson, 2003], v. 2, 902, 03).

Furthermore, J. Ramsey Michaels notes: "The context shows that Jesus has in mind primarily a moral example. But a liturgical example (i.e., that the disciples in their worship should literally act out the symbolism of the footwashing) is by no means excluded. This is especially true in light of the fact that, in this Gospel, the symbolic act of footwashing replaces the symbolic act of the institution of the Lord's Supper. Possibly John either knows of, or is advocating, the practice of footwashing in the Christian communities with which he is familiar. Such a practice would be a way for the Christian community to dramatize the responsibility of its members to be servants to one another and so to bring to full realization in the world the forgiveness and love of Jesus. It is not likely, however, that John intends an 'ordinance' or 'sacrament' of foot washing to displace the Lord's Supper at the center of Christian worship. His omission of the Lord's Supper is probably to be explained by the earlier inclusion of the synagogue discourse on the bread of life (esp. 6:52-58), which made an account of the institution superfluous. If John envisioned footwashing as a liturgical practice, he probably viewed it as part of what happened around the Lord's table, perhaps as a preparation for the Eucharist proper." J. Ramsey Michaels, *John* in the *New International Bible Commentary* (Peabody, Mass.: Hendrickson, 1989), 247. (Interestingly, the Brethren and Grace Brethren traditions view feet washing in this way, as a ritual preceding rather than following the Lord's Supper.)

7. Barclay, 469.

8. Ibid., 469-70. Barclay states what he thinks is the reason most Protestants hold to the Lord's Supper but not to the washing of feet: "The mere opinion of the *affirmers*, which by custom, education, and tradition, hath begotten in the hearts of people a greater reverence for, and esteem of the one than the other; which if it had fallen out to be as much recommended to us by tradition, would no doubt have been as tenaciously pleaded for, as having no less foundation in scripture."

9. Interestingly, this is more characteristic of low church, conservative bodies that are non-feet-washers (e.g., Presbyterians and Baptists). Most of Christendom has acknowledged that feet washing is a *liturgical act* to be observed in some form in the context of church worship. The difference is that most have not viewed it as a sacrament. (The Catholic and Eastern Orthodox churches have, however, viewed feet washing as a "sacramental"—an important liturgical act slightly less important than a full-fledged sacrament.)

10. I am using the phrase "non-feet-washers" out of convenience to refer to those who do not believe that feet washing is a Christian ordinance. Commentator Raymond Brown remarks that John 13:10 "is difficult if we rely on only a humility interpretation of the washing" (*The Gospel and Epistles of John: A Concise Commentary* [The Liturgical Press, 1988], 72).

11. See John Christopher Thomas, 11-18, who documents this. As Leon Morris states, "Many take the story as no more than a lesson in humility, quite overlooking the fact that, in that case, Jesus' dialogue with Peter completely obscures its significance! But those words, spoken in the shadow of the cross . . . have to do with cleansing" (Morris, 544). Similarly, A. M. Hunter asks, "Was the whole episode, as some hold, simply an acted out

parable whose theme was the glory of service? This is part of the truth, but far from the whole of it—or else in that mysterious dialogue with Peter Jesus is simply obscuring the parable's plain lesson." (*The Gospel According to John* in the *Cambridge Bible Commentaries on the New Testament* [Cambridge, England: Cambridge University Press, 1965], 134.)

JESUS, THE LORD, WHO BLED AND DIED

1. Je - sus, the Lord, who bled and died,
2. "Know you," He said, "what I have done?
3. See, through His robe, that glo - rious dress,
4. His wash - ing the dis - ci - ples' feet
5. With Christ our pat - tern thus in view,

A - ris - ing from His sup - per sweet,
You call me Lord and Mas - ter, too.
Which Christ in love laid hum - bly by:
Pro - claims His cleans - ing, heal - ing pow'r,
While we par - take His sup - per sweet,

Dis - robed, His gar - ments laid a - side, And
I have you an ex - am - ple shown. As
Clothed in a veil of mor - tal flesh, For
His re - as - sum - ing all com - plete, The
As He com - mands we'll joy - f'ly do, And

washed His dear dis - ci - ples' feet.
I have done, you ought to do."
man to suf - fer, bleed, and die.
great, the grand, tri - um - phant hour.
meek - ly wash each oth - er's feet.

from *Zion's Hymns*, 1854
L.M.

© 2006 by James M. Stevens
SHELLY

46

THE SYMBOLISM OF
FEET WASHING

Chapter Four

CHAPTER FOUR

In the last two chapters, we worked with Augustus H. Strong's definition of an ordinance, which we summarized as "outward rites Christ has appointed to be administered in His church, visible signs of the saving truth of the gospel that express it and confirm it in the believer." Again, while we do not acknowledge that this definition is necessary for a church practice to be an ordinance, let's play on our opponent's turf. In this chapter my main task is to answer the question, Does the washing of the saints' feet, to use Strong's words, symbolize the saving truth of the gospel?

TO "TYPIFY CHRIST"

The early Southern Baptist theologian John Leadley Dagg is one of the few people who has ever made a systematic argument against the washing of the saints' feet. The reason he believed he needed to make such an argument is probably that he was attempting to suppress feet washing among Southern Baptists. Remember that many Calvinistic Baptists, especially in rural areas, still practiced feet washing in the 1850s when Dagg was writing. As former president of Mercer University, he wanted to advocate the two ordinances of baptism and the Lord's Supper among Southern Baptists. So he was arguing not just against Free Will Baptists, but against many Calvinistic Baptists as to why the washing of the saints' feet should not be practiced as an ordinance in the church. In his book, *A Treatise of Church Order*, Dagg gives his main reason for not accepting feet washing as an ordinance: "It does not typify Christ."[1]

Again, let us keep in mind that to say that an ordinance must typify Christ is arbitrary. Scripture doesn't say that an ordinance has to typify Christ. In fact, Scripture does not say what an ordinance has to do. The New Testament, for example, commands the anointing of the sick with oil and the laying on of hands. These do not typify Christ, but the Holy Spirit and His ministry. However, as I have said, let us play ball in our opponent's court and ask whether feet washing symbolizes the saving truths of Christ and His gospel.

LOVE AND HUMBLE SERVICE

First of all, I believe that by examining John 13 we see that the washing of feet symbolizes love and humble service. Jesus' taking up the basin and towel to kneel at His disciples' feet and perform an act normally reserved for servants symbolizes love and humble service.[2] John reports Christ's humble act in the context of his statement that Jesus, "showed them the full extent of his love" (verse 1, NIV).[3] The apostle John tells us that Jesus showed His disciples the full extent of His love by washing their feet. He then commanded them to "do as I have done to you" (verse 15). It is no coincidence that, in this same context, Jesus tells His disciples, "Love one another, as I have loved you" (verse 34). In John 13, Jesus is teaching His disciples by example that real love for others does not sit idly; it kneels humbly to serve. The apostle Paul in Philippians 2:5-11 commends Jesus' example of self-giving, self-emptying love as He engages in the ultimate act of humility. Paul commands believers to:

> Let this mind be in you which was also in Christ Jesus, who, being in the form of God, did not consider it robbery to be equal with God, but made Himself of no rep-

utation, taking the form of a bondservant, and coming in the likeness of men. And being found in appearance as a man, He humbled Himself and became obedient to the point of death, even the death of the cross. Therefore God also has highly exalted Him and given Him the name which is above every name, that at the name of Jesus every knee should bow, of those in heaven, and of those on earth, and of those under the earth, and that every tongue should confess that Jesus Christ is Lord, to the glory of God the Father.

This picture of the humiliation and incarnation of Christ *lays the groundwork for our humility* in serving our brothers and sisters, in serving our fellow human beings. Jesus Christ wants us to have His mind. Because He was the suffering servant who gave Himself as the ransom for many, we must be suffering servants to our brothers and sisters. Love and humble service are not things that are incidental to the gospel message. They're not things that are peripheral to Jesus Christ, the redemptive significance of His life and death, and the message that He came to bring us. Love and humility are at the very heart and core of what Jesus was all about, at the center of the Christian gospel.[4]

A TWO-PRONGED GOSPEL

In Matthew 22:36, a Pharisee asks Jesus, "Teacher, which is the great commandment in the law?" Jesus' response is very instructive. He tells the man that there are two great commandments: "'You shall love the Lord your God with all your heart, with all your soul, and with all your mind.' This is the first and great commandment. And the second is like it: 'You shall love your neighbor as yourself'" (Matthew 22:37-39). You see, we have a *two-pronged gospel*. The gospel is not just about our relationship with God through Christ. It's also about a love for God that breaks out[5] into our relationship with others. It's a two-pronged gospel. The only way we can worship God truly, having the fellowship with God we so desperately need, is to have a reconciled relationship with our brothers and sisters.

The ordinance of feet washing is a vivid and beautiful symbol of this truth. It symbolizes the breaking out of our *vertical* relationship with God—this reconciled relationship we have with Him because of His Son Jesus Christ—into a reconciliation relationship with other people. The Lord's Supper is a symbol of our vertical relationship with God in Christ, what Christ did for us on the cross, our justification in Him, our reconciliation with Him. When we wash feet, we're symbolizing the breaking out of that relationship with God into our *horizontal* relationships with others.[6]

INDIVIDUALISM AND RECONCILIATION

It's not just "me and Jesus." Isn't that the individualistic message we hear in today's consumer-oriented evangelicalism? "Me and Jesus, we got our own thing goin'. Me and Jesus, we got it all worked out"—that's the gospel for many of us. You get saved. You are going to heaven to be with Jesus. That's the gospel. We've got our own thing going. We in evangelicalism have somehow lost sight of the fact that the gospel breaks out into a life that radically affects our lives and the lives of others for Jesus Christ. We have lost a reconciliation mentality in our gospel.

Feet washing teaches us that, yes, we have a right relationship with

God in Christ, who died for us and justifies us. But we also have sanctification, which produces love for each other. Our relationship with God breaks out into every area of our lives. It manifests itself publicly and profoundly in our love for one another. Love the Lord your God with all your heart, mind, soul, and strength. And love your neighbor as yourself.

We need ordinances that will teach us the two great commandments because Jesus goes on to say when He gives those commandments, "On these two commandments hang all the Law and the Prophets." It is not good enough to have the ordinance of the Lord's Supper, where we are talking about loving the Lord our God with all our heart, mind, soul, and strength, and just leave it at that. We must have an ordinance that represents, in the ritual life of the church, that we love our neighbors as ourselves.

> *In an upstairs room a parable*
> *Is just about to come alive.*
> *And while they bicker about who's best,*
> *With a painful glance He'll silently rise.*
> *Their savior servant must show them how*
> *By the will of the water and the tenderness of the towel.*
>
> *And the call is to community,*
> *The impoverished power that sets the soul free.*
> *In humility we take the vow*
> *That day after day we must take up the basin and the towel.*
>
> *And the space between ourselves sometimes*
> *Is more than the distance between the stars.*
> *By the fragile bridge of the servant's bow,*
> *We take up the basin and the towel.*[7]

The washing of the saints' feet can bring about spiritual and emotional healing in the body of Christ. So often relationships are healed through the ordinance of the washing of the saints' feet. That is what feet washing is all about. In the ritual life of the church, we need a symbolic reminder of the fact that our vertical relationship with God breaks out into our horizontal relationships with others, that our reconciliation relationship with God makes us reconcilers to other people. We need this desperately in the church. We need to recapture a sense of reconciliation, of being suffering servants to our brothers and sisters, of taking on the mind of Christ. Feet washing is a vivid pictorial symbol that expresses this truth.

There's a wonderful story from Howard Dorgan that illustrates this truth. Dorgan was a professor at Appalachian State University in Boone, North Carolina. He started going to Baptist churches in rural Appalachia, audio-taping their services and interviewing people. Soon he gathered enough information to write his excellent book, *Giving Glory to God in Appalachia: Worship Practices of Six Baptist Subdenominations*. He tells this story:

> Two women, both apparently in their late thirties or early forties, epitomized this entire service for me. The first of these women came to the front of the church to secure a basin and fill it with water. Her movements seemed slow, undecided, and troubled. When she turned back toward the congregation she hesitated a moment and then headed directly toward a second woman near the rear of the church. This second woman was noticeably agitated by the prospect of what was obviously about to happen. As the first knelt before the second and began to remove a shoe, their emotions burst forth with a force that suggested release from

months-perhaps years-of interpersonal tension. I do not know what problem had existed between these two, but I felt that I was watching the purgation of a malevolent spirit or a deeply embedded pain. During the remainder of the service the two were never separated. They clung to each other as if fearing a return to the same state of interpersonal torment which they both had hated.

Nor did the service allow me to escape without a challenge to my role as objective observer. I had just finished adjusting my tape recorder, when I discovered an elderly gentleman standing in front of me with towel and basin. "Can I wash your feet?" he said.

For a moment I was really without words, but then I managed to mumble something like, "No thank you. I really appreciate it, but. . . ."

Still he persisted: "I really wouldn't mind." But I had already declined and stuck to that decision. "I have to watch the recorder," I said, recognizing at the moment of speaking the lameness of my excuse. And the elderly gentleman turned and moved to a communicant sitting nearby.

On our way home that afternoon, after a traditional "dinner on the ground" feast served from tables supported by sawhorses, I couldn't help feeling somewhat disappointed in myself, particularly when my graduate assistant remarked, "I got my feet washed today." Would it have been all that discomfiting to have my feet washed by that kindly gentleman?

I also tried to imagine myself washing his feet, or anybody's feet, or the feet of any of those few professors at my university whom I considered my professional adversaries. I kept recalling an encounter session I had gone through back in the early 1970s when such sessions were in vogue, an affair in which all participants were supposed to "open up" and then learn to trust and empathize with each other. It occurred to me that a "good ol' fashion" footwashing might have been as effective, if not more so.[8]

INCARNATION

The reason love and humility are so tied to the gospel, and the reason the washing of the saints' feet is a Christ-typifying ordinance, is that it is rooted in the very incarnation and humiliation of Jesus Christ. Traditionally, theologians have referred to the incarnation of Christ as His humiliation. He came to serve. He came to give Himself up for us. Read from Philippians again:

> Let this mind be in you which was also in Christ Jesus, who, being in the form of God, did not consider it robbery to be equal with God, but made Himself of no reputation, taking the form of a bondservant, *and* coming in the likeness of men. And being found in appearance as a man, He humbled Himself and became obedient to *the point of* death, even the death of the cross (Philippians 2:5-8).

Does feet washing typify Jesus Christ? If feet washing does not typify Christ, I do not think there is anything in Scripture that could. I think it is the most beautiful and vivid symbol of Christ's condescension to us in all of Scripture. In that feet washing ceremony, Jesus rises up from supper and He takes off His cloak. He is laying aside the splendor of deity—the glory of heaven (verse 6).[9] He is removing that as one would a cloak. Then He takes upon Himself the form of a servant (verse 7). He takes the towel and He girds Himself with the towel as though girding Himself with our humanity (verse 8a). He kneels to serve us (verse 8b). Disrobed of all His heavenly dress, the God of the universe kneels to serve me, to die for me (verse 8c).[10]

Does feet washing typify Christ? I believe it does. It typifies Christ in His incarnation and in His humiliation as a suffering servant come to condescend to our low estate—to serve us and to die for us. The washing of the saints' feet typifies the incarnation of Christ in a beautiful, pictorial, symbolic way. That's why we say that feet washing is about humility—because Jesus is all about humility. He humbled Himself and became obedient to the death of the cross. You cannot be crucified daily until you humble yourself like Jesus did, until you are characterized by humiliation. That is why we need this ritual in the life of the church: to symbolize for us, to express for us, and to confirm in us the humiliation of Jesus Christ and how it comes into our lives and radically transforms us as we are conformed to His image.

SANCTIFICATION

I have discussed love and humble service as well as incarnation and humiliation. There is one more way that the washing of the saints' feet symbolizes the saving truths of the gospel: sanctification, cleansing from sin. Look again at John 13:8-11:

> Peter said to Him, "You shall never wash my feet!"
>
> Jesus answered him, "If I do not wash you, you have no part with Me."
>
> Simon Peter said to Him, "Lord, not my feet only, but also my hands and my head!"
>
> Jesus said to Him, "He who is bathed needs only to wash his feet, but is completely clean; and you are clean, but not all of you."

If Jesus was not trying to get something across here, then why did He go to so much trouble? Jesus tells Peter that if He does not wash Peter's feet, Peter will have no part with Him. Then Peter asks Jesus to wash not only his feet but also his hands and his head. Jesus responds that the disciples' bodies are already clean and do not need to be washed again. Only their feet need to be washed. He notes in passing that one of the disciples (Judas) is not clean. What does Jesus mean here? Jesus is telling Peter, and He is telling us, that feet washing symbolizes daily cleansing of sin, which is a necessary part of sanctification. Jesus said, "'He who is bathed needs only to wash his feet, but is completely clean; and you are clean, but not all of you.' For He knew who would betray Him; therefore He said, 'You are not all clean'" (verses 10, 11). All the disciples except Judas, Jesus said, had their bodies washed—this is a symbol of justification. Yet they still needed to have their feet washed—this is a symbol of sanctification.

A growing number of modern biblical scholars believe that the phrase "he who is bathed needs only to wash his feet, but is completely clean" (John 13:10) refers to baptism and salvation: You do not need your whole body washed—that is the symbol of baptism, which is symbolizing justification. But you need your feet washed.[11] This is symbolizing sanctification or cleansing from sin—forgiveness of post-baptismal sin, as John Christopher Thomas says in his book.[12] As William Hendriksen remarks, Jesus is saying that

> he who is bathed—that is, he who has been cleansed by my blood (justified)—has no need of washing anything *except his feet.* . . . that is, such a person being cleaned altogether (all his sins having been forgiven) needs only *one* thing, namely sanctification, here especially (though not exclusively) that work of God within the heart whereby the believer attains constantly renewed and

ever-growing humility and day by day willingness and eagerness to render service to others in gratitude for all the benefits received.[13]

Feet washing symbolizes this cleansing from sin and the resulting growth in holiness and conformity to the will of Jesus Christ. This is a saving truth of the gospel if ever there were one.

Leroy Forlines in his Romans commentary argues eloquently that justification and sanctification go hand-in-hand.[14] You can't have one without the other. We were buried with Christ (justification) so that we might be raised with Christ (sanctification). This growth in Christlikeness, this daily cleansing from sin, is at the core of the gospel, which says that Christ came to grant us His righteousness so that we might be freed to practice personal righteousness and flee from sin.

This is the object of the work of Christ in our lives. God did not send Jesus Christ to die for us just so we could be justified and go to heaven. He sent Christ so we might be conformed to His image. Salvation is not just being saved and baptized so that you have your ticket on the gospel train. It's not fire insurance. It's something much deeper—more life-changing and wonderful and beautiful. The gospel truth of sanctification is most vividly expressed and confirmed in the believer in the washing of the saints' feet.

CONCLUSION

Understanding that feet washing symbolizes love and humble service, the humiliation and incarnation of Christ, and sanctification refutes the objection that it does not qualify as an ordinance because it does not typify Christ or symbolize the saving truth of the gospel.[15] This understanding also answers the objection that, in washing their feet, Jesus was giving them a lesson in humility to be taken figuratively and lived out in daily acts of humility. The washing of the saints' feet is a ritual symbol of love and humble service, which grows out of the incarnation and humiliation of Christ, and we understand that as our relationship with God through Christ breaks out in all of life, it changes the way we live. We are cleansed from sin and set on a new path of holy living and conformity to the image of Christ.

NOTES

1. John Leadley Dagg, *A Treatise of Church Order* (originally pub. 1858. Repr. Harrisonburg, Va.: Gano, 1990), 229.

2. This phrase is from Merrill C. Tenney, "The Gospel of John," in *The Expositor's Bible Commentary* (Grand Rapids: Zondervan, 1971), 9:137. See also his *John: The Gospel of Belief* (Grand Rapids: Eerdmans, 1948). John Christopher Thomas, like numerous commentators he cites in his work, ties feet washing to love and humble service as well: "There can be no doubt that footwashing was the domain of slaves. . . . There is so much an identification of servants and footwashing that the footbasin comes to function figuratively as a sign of servitude. . . . In John 13 such service issuing from love is evident, both from the emphasis on servitude and also from the prominence given in v. 1 to Jesus' own love for his own" (Thomas, 88). As J. Ramsey Michaels has said, feet washing "is both a symbol and a concrete expression of self-giving love. To wash one another's feet (v. 14) is to 'love one another.'" (*John* in the *New International Bible Commentary* [Peabody, Mass.: Hendrickson, 1989], 241.)

3. The New King James Version reads: "Having loved His own who were in the world, He loved them to the end."

4. Leon Morris contends that the feet washing account is "a parable in action, setting out that great principle of lowly service which brings cleansing and which finds its supreme embodiment in the cross, setting out also the necessity for the disciple to take the Lord's way, not his own" (Morris, 544).

5. This phrase from the sixteenth-century Anabaptist theologian Balthasar Hubmaier has had a great impact on my thought on spirituality. Hubmaier, for example, says in his *Eighteen Articles* of April 1524 that faith "cannot remain passive but must break out

[*aussbrechen*] to God in thanksgiving and to mankind in all kinds of works of brotherly love" (*Balthasar Hubmaier: Schriften*, ed. Gunnar Westin and Torsten Bertgsten, v. 9 of *Quellen zur Geschichte der Taufer*, [Gutersloh: Verlagshaus Gerd Mohn, 1962], 72; quoted in William R. Estep, *Renaissance and Reformation* [Grand Rapids: Eerdmans, 1986], 208).

6. Several modern commentators suggest that the feet washing in John 13 is symbolic, at least in part, of Christ's death on the cross. (See John Christopher Thomas' list of such commentators on pg.16) Yet they tend to suggest that this does not obscure Christ's teaching of the need for the disciples' humble service to others. As Christ humbled Himself becoming obedient to the point of death (Philippians 2:8), so the disciples should humble themselves, being willing to serve others even to the point of laying down their lives for others (John 15:12, 13). Thus, even while one might not see Christ's death as the chief symbol in the feet washing narrative, this symbolism does not contradict the fact that feet washing is emblematic of love and humble service. Rather, it strongly supports the concept. See Raymond E. Brown, *The Gospel of John* in the *Anchor Bible* (Garden City: Doubleday, 1963), 2:569.

7. Michael Card, "The Basin and the Towel," from the CD *Scribbling in the Sand*. © Birdwing Music.

8. Howard Dorgan, *Giving Glory to God in Appalachia: Worship Practices of Six Baptist Subdenominations* (Knoxville: University of Tennessee Press, 1987), 121-22. After reiterating several feet washing services he witnessed in his travels among the Baptists of Appalachia, Dorgan commented, "As in the incident of the two women at Silas Creek, on several occasions I felt I was watching acts of interpersonal reconciliation or renewal. There were moments of impassioned breakthrough, when the holding back was finally over; and there were scenes of abject contrition and humility, as individual bathers bent low over feet that had toes intensely curled. The reward afterwards, however, was always a genuinely warm embrace" (146).

N. T. Wright, Bishop of Durham in the Church of England, emphasizes the emotional intimacy of washing someone else's feet: "The first time I did it, I had prepared for the service in the usual way. But nothing could have prepared me for the sense of holy intimacy that went with the simple but profound action of washing other people's feet. . . . Washing them is both very mundane . . . and very close and personal. Washing between someone else's toes is an intimate action. It is a moment of tenderness" N.T. Wright, *John for Everyone: Chapters 11-21*, (Louisville, Ky: Westminster John Knox, 2004), 43.

9. I do not mean to say here that Jesus is laying aside His glory, etc., at this moment or on this occasion. Rather, I am using figures of speech to discuss what He is graphically *symbolizing* for His disciples.

10. The view that the feet washing represents the incarnation is a traditional interpretation found in such interpreters as Augustine (see Appendix Two), John Calvin, Matthew Henry, John Gill, and David Brown, as well as in myriad modern interpreters. D. A. Carson, for example, says, "Thus he began to wash the disciples' feet, thereby demonstrating the claim, 'I am among you as one who serves' (Luke. 22:27; cf. Mark 10:45 par.). The one who was 'in very nature God . . . made himself nothing'

and took 'the very nature of a servant' (Phil. 2:6-7). Indeed, he became obedient to death—even death on a cross! (Phil. 2:8)." (*The Gospel According to John* in the *Pillar New Testament Commentary* [Grand Rapids: Eerdmans, 1991], 463.) Cf. F. F. Bruce's statement: "John's graphic description illustrates the statement of Phil. 2:6f. . . . In the washing of their feet the disciples, though they did not understand it at the time, saw a rare unfolding of the authority and glory of the incarnate Word, and a rare declaration of the character of the Father himself." (*The Gospel of John* [Grand Rapids: Eerdmans, 1983], 280.) As William Hendrickson says, "Phil. 2:7 'taking the form of a servant' comes to our mind immediately. . . . Truly, the Lord of glory had 'girded himself with humility'" (229). See also Gerald L. Borchert, *John 12-21* in the *New American Commentary* (Nashville: Broadman & Holman, 2002), 79, and Wright (45). I like what Joseph F. Ryan says when he states: "When He takes His outer clothes off He is laying aside His glory as the Son of God. It reminds us of the Christmas carol line, 'Mild he lays his glory by. . . . 'Don't miss this. It is the incarnation." (*That You May Believe: Studies in the Gospel of John* by Joseph F. Ryan. Copyright © 2003, 295. Used by permissions of Crossway Books, a ministry of Good News Publishers, Wheaton, IL 60187, www.crossway.com.)

"Disrobed of all his heavenly dress" is an allusion to the hymn "He Washed His Servants' Feet." (*Rejoice: The Free Will Baptist Hymn Book*, 1988.) This hymn was originally in Rufus K. Hearn, Joseph S. Bell, and Jesse Randolph, *Zion's Hymns: For the Use of the Original Free-Will Baptist Church of North Carolina, and for the Saints of All Denominations* (Pikeville, N.C.: Elder Daniel Davis, 1854).

11. Allen Edgington remarks: "Without introduction, Jesus moves to the spiritual level when he declares that they are all clean except Judas, who is unregenerate. On the physical level, the bath makes one clean. On the spiritual level regeneration makes one clean; 'the washing referred to is wholly spiritual. It is that of regeneration and renewing, regarded as one concept.' On the physical level, one washes only his dirty feet after walking—a complete bath is unnecessary. On the spiritual level, believers are defiled daily by sin as they 'walk' in this sinful world—another 'bath' is not necessary, though they need the daily cleansing which comes from recognizing sin and confessing it. This is what is meant by 'having part with him,' viz., participating daily in intimate fellowship with him. Christ in his present ministry of sanctification is applying the Word to believers and there by cleansing them—a truth taught expressly later that evening (John 15:2, 3; 17:17)" (Edgington, 429-30).

12. Thomas, 14-15, 98-107. This was the view of Augustine as well (See Appendix Two). Mark Edwards remarks: "Augustine warns that, while the whole of a man is bathed in his unrepeatable baptism, the feet of Peter represent the abiding sins of the flesh." (*John* in the *Blackwell Bible Commentaries*. [Oxford, England: Blackwell, 2004], 132). I need to state here that I hold the traditional, longer reading of John 13:10, rather than the shorter reading of many modern critical scholars, which omits "needs only to wash his feet." Still, a host of modern scholars, especially conservatives, retain the longer reading (e.g., E. W. Hengstenberg, Alvay Hovey, B. F. Westcott, Marcus Dods, Merrill Tenney, Charles Erdman, R. C. H. Lenski, A. M. Hunter, Ernst Haenchen, Walter Lüthi, Everett F. Harrison, John Christopher Thomas, Craig Keener, Bruce Milne, D. A. Carson, J. Carl Laney, Charles Talbert, Joseph Ryan, William Hendriksen, et al.). I

concur with J. Ramsey Michaels, who sums up the position of these commentators: "These words [except for his feet] are omitted in one ancient Greek manuscript, but the vast majority of manuscripts, including the most ancient, preserve the longer reading. . . . It is better to follow the lead of the best manuscripts (as NIV has done) and adopt the longer reading, with its implication that the footwashing represents not the initial *bath* but a second cleansing. . . ." (J. Ramsey Michaels, *John* in the *New International Bible Commentary* [Peabody, Mass.: Hendrickson, 1989], 246.)

13. William Hendriksen, *The Gospel of John* (Grand Rapids: Baker, 1953), 233. Cf. Alvah Hovey's comment: ". . . this process of daily sanctification, by which believers are continued in fellowship with Christ, is here symbolized by washing the feet" (*Commentary on the Gospel of John* [Valley Forge, Penn.: Judson, repr. {1885}, 269) and that of John Peter Lange: "The maxim generalized reads thus for Christians; Justification must be followed by sanctification or daily repentance." (*The Gospel of John* in *Commentary on the Holy Scriptures*, Trans. and ed. Philip Schaff [Grand Rapids: Zondervan repr. {1871}, 409.) This is the view of the vast majority of traditional commentators, as well as most modern commentators who accept the longer reading of John 13:10 (see, e.g., such commentators as John Calvin, Matthew Henry, Matthew Poole, John Gill, Heinrich Meyer, E. W. Hengstenberg, John Charles Ellicott, B. F. Westcott, Marcus Dods, R. C. H. Lenski, Merrill Tenney, Everett F. Harrison, Bruce Milne, J. Ramsey Michaels, D. A. Carson, and J. Carl Laney).

14. F. Leroy Forlines, *Romans* in the *Randall House Bible Commentary* (Nashville: Randall House, 1987), 146-58.

15. I have wondered in the past, when preaching this passage, could Jesus have really been symbolizing all these things? He really seems to be doing so. I was encouraged in my interpretation by D. A. Carson who, two pages after a lengthy discussion of how Jesus' washing of the disciples' feet is a picture of His incarnation, says that it has three "applications": (1) It symbolizes "Christ's atoning, cleansing death." (2) It shows that "individuals who have been cleansed by Christ's atoning work will doubtless need to have subsequent sins washed away." (3) It "teaches lessons in humility" (Carson, 465). See also Leon Morris's comment on the multi-faceted symbolism of the feet washing narrative (Morris, 544). Joseph F. Ryan argues that the washing of the disciples' feet symbolizes all three (Ryan, 295-97). One also sees an affirmation of the multi-faceted symbolism of the John 13 narrative in commentators such as William Hendriksen, Merrill Tenney, Ernst Haenchen, and J. Carl Laney.

Emblems of Thy Condescension

1. Once the gra-cious Lord of glo-ry Laid His earth-ly robes a-side,
2. He who claimed no rep-u-ta-tion Laid His heaven-ly robes a-side,
3. Grant, O Sav-ior, that Thy crea-tures, Gaz-ing on Thy love-ly face,
4. Em-blems of Thy con-de-scen-sion Will-ing-ly we take up now

Took a ba-sin filled with wa-ter, 'Round His waist a tow-el tied;
Took man's sin-ful like-ness on Him Will-ing-ly and free-ly died;
May in low-li-ness be-fore Thee Bow and take a ser-vant's place;
And with ser-vant's cloth and ba-sin Low be-fore our breth-ren bow;

Knelt in ten-der-ness be-fore them, His hu-mil-i-ty com-plete,
Lived the Son of Man a-mong us, Stained His beau-ty for all men,
May Thy heaven-ly grace sus-tain us, Our hu-mil-i-ty com-plete,
Grant that as we kneel be-fore them, Hearts of self may emp-tied be,

And with gen-tle, kind com-pas-sion Bathed His own dis-ci-ples' feet.
Yield-ed, as the Fa-ther made Him Sin for us, who knew no sin.
Thy mind rest-ing now with-in us As we kneel at Thy dear feet.
As we take Thy like-ness on us, Ev-er filled with on-ly Thee.

Mary Ruth Wisehart
8.7.8.7.D.

Leavitt's *The Christian Lyre*, 1831
Attr. to Wolfgang A. Mozart, 1756-1791
Arr. by Hubert P. Main, c. 1868
ELLESDIE

FEET WASHING OUTSIDE
THE GOSPELS

Chapter Five

CHAPTER FIVE

For something to be an ordinance, does it have to be mentioned outside the gospels? Many who do not practice feet washing as an ordinance argue that it does not qualify as an ordinance because it is not mentioned outside the gospels—in the Acts or the epistles. This begs the question. Where does one infer this principle from the Old or New Testaments?

I believe that the washing of the saints' feet *is* mentioned outside the gospels in 1 Timothy 5. But I do not believe that a practice or ordinance has to be mentioned outside the gospels to be valid for the church today. This is demonstrated simply by looking at other essential church practices that are not mentioned in the Acts or the letters.

THE TRINITARIAN FORMULA AND CHURCH DISCIPLINE

While I was in college working on a study project, a friend and I went to a United Pentecostal church—a "oneness" Pentecostal church that believed in "Jesus only." The preacher was preaching right at me and my friend. He knew we were strangers. He said, "I've got the keys to a Winnebago in my pocket, and I'll give the keys to that Winnebago to anyone in the congregation who can show me where the apostles baptized in the name of anyone but Jesus." The "Jesus only" Pentecostal argument is that the church should not baptize in the name of the Father, Son, and Holy Spirit. The apostles didn't do it. It wasn't mentioned in the epistles. It wasn't mentioned in the book of Acts. The church should baptize in the name of Jesus only. That is what the apostles did. So that is the doctrine of the apostles, they argue.

The Trinitarian baptismal formula is mentioned only in the Great Commission in Matthew 28:19: "Go therefore and make disciples of all the nations, baptizing them in the name of the Father and of the Son and of the Holy Spirit. . . ." Jesus says, "Baptize in the name of the Father, Son, and Holy Spirit." Yet this preacher had the keys to a Winnebago, and he was ready to give me those keys if I could show him one place in the Acts or the epistles where the apostles used the Trinitarian formula in baptism. Obviously I could not do that, because he was right—the apostolic use of the Trinitarian formula in baptism is not recorded in the Acts or the epistles. But does anyone really believe that principle of interpretation? It is the same argument many non-feet-washers use against the practice of feet washing as an ordinance. They say that one must show them somewhere outside the gospels where the apostles actually practiced it. Do they really believe that one has to do that? No, because then they would have to be "Jesus only."

There is another example of a universally acknowledged church practice that is commanded by Christ in the gospels but not mentioned in the Acts or the epistles. The church discipline procedure Jesus commanded in Matthew 18 is not mentioned in either the Acts or letters. Yet no one would argue that the procedure is not authoritative for the church simply because it is mentioned only once in the gospels. It seems obvious that for something to be practiced in the church, it does not have to be mentioned or practiced outside the gospels. Christ's command in the gospels is sufficient.

To say that feet washing has to be mentioned in the epistles or in Acts to be considered an ordinance is a delimiting definition of ordinance. As I argued in chapter two, the Bible does not define *ordinance.* The only way that the New Testament defines ordinance is as something that is ordained by God to be perpetuated in the church. We don't have any clues from Scripture that something the church should practice should be commanded not only in the gospels, but also in the Acts and the letters.

THE LORD'S SUPPER OUTSIDE THE GOSPELS

The only uncontested mention of the Lord's Supper itself is in 1 Corinthians, and that was only because of controversy and abuse. The only reason Paul brought up the Lord's Supper was because the Corinthian church had abused the ordinance and there was controversy over its practice. So Paul addressed this concern and controversy. Otherwise, there would be no mention of the Lord's Supper in the epistles. Some scholars try to assert that the breaking of bread from house to house that we see twice in Acts is the Lord's Supper. But many scholars convincingly argue that the phrase does not refer to the Lord's Supper. Rather, it has to do with sharing common meals in the context of church *koinonia.* So, even the Lord's Supper would not have been viewed as an ordinance, according to the above criterion, if the Corinthians had not abused it.

THE WASHING OF THE SAINTS' FEET IN 1 TIMOTHY 5

It makes sense to see Jesus' command of a particular practice as ample warrant for obeying that command. However, I believe the washing of the saints' feet *is* mentioned in 1 Timothy 5:9, 10. In fact, that is where we get the phrase "washing the saints' feet." It says:

> Do not let a widow under sixty years old be taken into
> the number, and not unless she has been the wife of one
> man, well reported for good works: if she has brought
> up children, if she has lodged strangers, if she has
> washed the saints' feet, if she has relieved the afflicted, if
> she has diligently followed every good work.

Many scholars believe that this roll of widows is a sort of office in the early church, a kind of female equivalent of the office of deacon, and that these widows were placed on an official roll, to help and serve in the local congregation. Many commentators, like Raymond E. Brown and Elizabeth Schussler Fiorenza, argue that this passage is talking about the literal ritual of the washing of the saints' feet. Brown states: "That the practice [of feet washing in John 13] was taken seriously is attested in 1 Timothy v. 10 where one of the qualifications for a woman to be enrolled as a widow is that she have shown hospitality and have 'washed the feet of the saints.'"[1]

Those who don't believe that feet washing is a literal church ritual say that this phrase in chapter five of 1 Timothy, "has washed the saints' feet," is just another way of symbolizing hospitality. In other words, when a stranger comes to the door, this widow washes his feet. They've got dirt on them, and she washes feet to get the dirt off. So they say this is just another way of symbolizing hospitality.

John Christopher Thomas provides four reasons why this interpretation is implausible. First, the other examples of good works in this passage refer to distinct actions that are *different* from one another: brought up children, shown hospitality, washed the saints' feet, helped those in trouble, devoted herself to every good work. It makes sense, he says, to see feet washing as a distinct kind of good work different from hospitality. The question he raises is, why would the apostle say "hospitable," and then repeat that, if he is only talking about *another kind* of hospitality to strangers. She has shown hospitality; she has washed the saints' feet. If Paul is not talking about a religious act, he is being redundant. Why?

Second, Thomas says, "The mention of footwashing in a list of duties is a rarity. For although footwashing was generally the domain of servants," lists of duties found in that time fail to mention washing feet.[2] The other duties listed in this passage are commonly mentioned in lists of responsibilities or duties found in the ancient world at this time. But feet washing, even washing the feet of strangers, is never mentioned in these lists. So Thomas concludes that this is an indication of a ritual, religious act.

The third reason he gives for why the reference to feet washing here is not just another way of signifying hospitality is that free women would not have washed the feet of guests. Only slaves would have.

Fourth, if feet washing is just another word for hospitality in this verse, why does it call for widows who have washed only *saints'* feet? Why would she not wash non-saints' feet? Why is the widows' feet washing "restricted to the household of faith" if indeed the washing of the saints' feet is just a euphemism for hospitality?[3] As Thomas has suggested, there is every good reason to believe that in 1 Timothy 5:10 the widows had engaged in a *religious* observance of washing of the saints' feet, not a mere act of hospitality.[4]

THE CHURCH FATHERS AND FEET WASHING

If we had the command of Christ to wash feet in John 13 and the widows' feet washing qualification in 1 Timothy 5, and had no existing records of the ritual washing of feet in early Christianity outside the Bible, we would still have warrant to practice it. Because Christ commanded it, the church would need to practice it. But the case for feet washing is strengthened when we see how widespread a literal reading of feet washing was among the church fathers.[5]

A large number of people in early Christianity talked about the washing of feet, not as a figurative observance of feet washing in daily acts of humility, but as the liturgical or ritual practice in a religious service of the washing of the saints' feet.[6] While there are a number of prominent church fathers who advocated the literal, ritual practice of feet washing in the church, we will discuss only three here.

Tertullian

Around A.D. 211, Tertullian argued for the literal practice of feet washing:

> I must recognize Christ, both as He reclines on a couch, and when He presents a basin for the feet of His disciples, and when he pours water into it from a ewer, and when He is gird about with a linen towel. . . . It is thus in general that I reply upon the point admitting indeed that *we use along with others these articles. . . .*[7]

Ambrose

Ambrose of Milan wrote a great deal about the washing of feet in the fourth century A.D. In one passage, he complained that the church in Rome had stopped observing the custom of feet washing. The following quotation shows that Ambrose himself observed the washing of the saints' feet as a religious ritual in the Milanese church. But he is chiding the church in Rome for having once observed the ritual and abandoning it. He says, "We are not ignorant that the Church of Rome has not this custom. This custom of washing feet she does not retain. Behold, therefore, perhaps she has declined from the practice on account of the multitude." A lot of people are coming into the Church of Rome and perhaps this is why she has declined from the practice, because it's too hard to keep doing it. He goes on to say,

> There are some truly who endeavor to excuse her by the plea that this custom is not a sacred rite, but it is simply to be done to our guests as a mark of hospitality, but it is one thing to perform an act in token of humility and another thing to perform it in order to sanctification. Hear therefore how we prove this to be a sacred rite in order to sanctification. "Unless I wash thy feet, thou hast no part with me." I do not thus speak that I may censure others, but that I may commend my office. I desire in all things to follow the Roman church, but nevertheless, we men have sense also and therefore what is more correctly practiced elsewhere in the church, we are more correct in practicing. In this respect we follow the Apostolic Peter himself. We adhere to the example of his devotion. For truly Peter the Apostle is our authority for this assertion. Peter himself said, "Lord, not my feet only but my hands and my head."[8]

By this time Ambrose is attaching a really important significance to Peter. The fact that Peter was the one who debated with Jesus about feet washing and soon enthusiastically accepted it was more significant for Ambrose than if it had occurred with any of the other disciples. Ambrose's commitment to the literal practice of feet washing is seen no more vividly than in the following passage, in which he again ties the washing of feet both to humility and cleansing from sin:

I, then, wish also myself to wash the feet of my brethren, I wish to fulfill the commandment of my Lord, I will not be ashamed in myself, nor disdain what He Himself did first. Good is the mystery of humility, because while washing pollution of others I wash away my own.[9]

Augustine

Lastly, even as late as the fifth century, Augustine not only mentioned the literal practice of washing feet but argued that it is sacramental in nature. "As to the feet washing, . . . the question has arisen as to what time it is best by *literal performance* of this work to give public instruction in the important duty which it illustrates."[10] In his *Lectures and Tactates on the Gospel, According to St. John*, Augustine actually refers to the washing of feet as "a sacramental sign."[11] His comments further indicate that he is committed not only to what the washing of feet is a figure of, but also to its literal practice:

And wherever such is not in practice among the saints, what they do not do with the hand they do in heart. . . . But it is far better, and beyond all dispute more accordant with the truth that *it should also be done with the hands;* nor should the Christian think it beneath him to do what was done by Christ. For when the body is bent at a brother's feet, the feeling of such humility is either awakened in the heart itself, or is strengthened if already present.[12]

These are just three opinions chosen from myriad authors in early Christianity who practiced the washing of the saints' feet literally as a liturgical rite. This observance influenced the later church, as is evidenced by the practice of feet washing throughout the history of both the Roman Catholic and Eastern Orthodox churches.

What are we to make of these references? If we had no evidence from Scripture, I don't think these quotations from the church fathers would be of much help to us. After all, there were many practices that arose in the church very early that had no scriptural warrant whatever. The surviving evidence of the literal practice of feet washing in the early church shows, at least, that the community that originally read and interpreted John's gospel believed and taught the literal practice of feet washing, and that this interpretation survived in diverse segments of early Christianity.[13] I believe these fathers' opinions strengthen our case for the ritual observance of feet washing in the life of the church.

NOTES

1. *The Gospel According to John.* 2 vols; (Garden City: Doubleday, 1966-70), 2:569. Cf. Elizabeth Schussler Fiorenza, *In Memory of Her* (New York: Crossroad, 1994), 324. C. K. Barrett and Donald Guthrie also tie the widows' washing of the saints' feet to Christ's ceremony in John 13, rather than to mere cultural custom (C. K. Barrett, *The Pastoral Epistles* [Oxford: Clarendon, 1963], 76; Donald Guthrie, *The Pastoral Epistles* [Grand Rapids: Eerdmans, 1957], 103-04). John Christopher Thomas (136-37) shows that the view that 1 Timothy 5:10 reflects a tradition based on John 13, not mere hospitable custom, is strong among British and continental European scholars (e.g., Barrett, Guthrie, N. J. D. White, J. N. D. Kelley, Herman Ridderbos, C. P. Spicq, Marie-Joseph Lagrange, Bernhard Kotting, Norbert Brox, Gottfried Holtz, Udo Borse, and Jurgen Roloff). Augustine clearly believed that 1 Timothy 5:10 was referring to the literal practice of feet washing. (See Appendix Two.)

2. Thomas, 135.

3. Ibid.; See also Homer Kent, *The Pastoral Epistles* (Chicago: Moody, 1958), 173; Stanley Outlaw, *1 Timothy* in the *Randall House Bible Commentary* (Nashville: Randall House, 1990), 259-60; E. F. Scott, *The Pastoral Epistles* (London: Hodder and Stoughton, 1936), p. 61; D. Edmond Hiebert, *First Timothy* (Chicago: Moody, 1957). Allen Edgington explains: "Nor is this to be understood as a display of humility accomplished through the performance of a social custom. If this were so it would be difficult to understand why 'the saints' are specifically mentioned. 'Hospitality' and 'washed' are not to be taken as parallel references to unbelievers and believers, respectively. The first phrase (translated 'showing hospitality' by the NIV) need not refer only to strangers. Even if 'strangers' are in view, one believer who is unknown to another could qualify as a 'stranger,' since many believers were traveling missionaries and evangelists"

(Edgington, 432-33). Tertullian also separates women's washing the saints' feet from general acts of hospitality. In a list of duties performed by Christian women, Tertullian mentions a number of hospitable acts alongside both the Lord's Supper and washing of the saints' feet (see Thomas, 140; Edgington, 433).

4. My colleague Darrell Holley recently offered a perspective that I think is enlightening and on-target: "This clause ('if she have washed the saints' feet') appears after two very concrete actions ('brought up children' and 'lodged strangers') and before two rather abstract images ('relieved the afflicted' and 'have diligently followed every good work'). The clause's use here appears to me to be in the same abstract nature as the latter two. If so, this in no way lessens the reference of this text to feetwashing as a rite in the primitive churches. Indeed, if this clause is used as a metaphor for 'serving others,' such usage would make sense only within a [milieu] where feetwashing was a common image for servanthood. Does this not seem to indicate that feetwashing as a literal ceremonial rite was a common practice within the churches, so common that the term could be used metaphorically?" (private communication). Cf. Thomas, 135-37.

5. I must make clear what I am and am *not* trying to prove by these examples from the church fathers. First, what we see here is just that regular, ritual feet washing as a literal, liturgical practice in the church was being practiced by a number of notable church fathers. Thus, it cannot be argued that feet washing merely arose in the sixteenth century with the Anabaptists, without precedent in church history. Another way of putting it is that many early Christians interpreted feet washing as a regular, literal activity in church just as modern-day Anabaptists, Free Will Baptists, etc., do. This is significant. What I am not saying here is that feet washing is universally acknowledged by the church fathers as a sacrament. (As I argue in Appendix One, the church fathers disagreed among themselves on the definition, nature, and number of the sacraments.)

Some people who object to feet washing worry that the fact that the church fathers or the medieval church did not universally view feet washing as a sacrament (on the level with baptism, the Eucharist, confirmation, penance, matrimony, holy orders, or extreme unction) strikes a fatal blow to seeing it as a literal church ordinance. This reasoning is flawed in two ways: First, all of Protestant Christianity differs strongly from the sacramental views of most of the fathers and medieval theologians, both Eastern Orthodox and Western Catholic, and in many cases the Eastern Orthodox and Western Catholic traditions seem to align more with the views of the majority of the church fathers than does the Protestant tradition. This is precisely why Protestants have never relied on "the universal consent of the fathers" as a norm for formulating and teaching doctrine.

This leads to the second flaw in this argument: There are numerous free church doctrines for which there is little or no evidence in Patristic literature. That is why Anabaptists and Baptists have always claimed to go to the New Testament for their views on the church. Thus, we argue, for example, that only believers are to be baptized, that baptism is only by immersion, that congregations are self-governing and not ruled by a bishop who oversees several local churches, that the words bishop, pastor, and elder all refer to the same office, that ordinances are symbols and do not actually convey grace. These views are grounded in the New Testament and are not universally affirmed by the church fathers. Yet we are content that these are biblical views and delighted that some of the church fathers share our position on them.

So I am not arguing that feet washing was universally practiced by the church fathers. Nor do I think we need evidence of the universal consent of the fathers for any church doctrine or practice. Just as it does not bother me that the majority of the Christian tradition has practiced infant baptism by aspersion (sprinkling) or adopted episcopal church government, so it does not bother me that the majority of the Christian tradition has not viewed feet washing as a sacrament. Yet it is very interesting to me that there were important church fathers who, like me, regularly practiced feet washing as a physical act in a worship setting.

6. See Thomas's extensive discussion of the church fathers and feet washing (126-86). An interesting indication that feet washing was widespread in the early churches is the fact that writers such as Ambrose, Augustine, and Origen would mention off-hand other churches and Christians who also practiced the washing of feet in some form or other. The fact that the Synod of Elvira in Spain saw fit to begin prohibiting the washing of feet of the newly baptized is in itself an indication that that practice was widespread.

7. *De Corona* 8, in Alexander Roberts and James Donaldson, eds., *Ante-Nicene Fathers* (Grand Rapids: Eerdmans, 1951), 3:98. (Italics added.)

8. *The Sacraments* 3.5, in R. J. Defarrari, trans., *Saint Ambrose: Theological and Dogmatic Works*; Washington: Catholic University Press of America, 1963, 291-92. Ambrose's statement here also shows that he believed that the washing of the saints' feet is not only about humility but also about sanctification.

9. *Of the Holy Spirit* 1.15, in Philip Schaff and Henry Wace, eds., *Nicene and Post-Nicene Fathers*, Series II, Grand Rapids: Eerdmans. 1955), 10:95.

10. *Letter* 55.33, in Philip Schaff, ed., *Nicene and Post-Nicene Fathers*, Series I (Grand Rapids: Eerdmans, 1952), 1:314. (Italics added.)

11. *Lectures and Tractates on the Gospel According to St. John* 58.5, in Schaff, ed., *Nicene and Post-Nicene Fathers*, Series I (Grand Rapids Eerdmans, 1956), 7:307. (Italics added.) Augustine states: "For what else does the Lord apparently intimate in the profound significance of this sacramental sign, when He says, 'For I have given you an example, that ye should do as I have done to you'; but what the apostle declares in the plainest terms, 'Forgiving one another, if any man have a quarrel against any: even as Christ forgave you, so also do ye'?"

12. *Lectures and Tractates on the Gospel According to St. John* 58.4, in Schaff, ed., *Nicene and Post-Nicene Fathers*, 7:306. Series I (Grand Rapids Eerdmans, 1956), 7:307. (Italics added.)

13. See Thomas, 127-47. It is noteworthy that liturgical feet washing is found in both linguistically and geographically diverse segments of early Christianity.

HE WASHED HIS SERVANTS' FEET

1. Dis - robed of all His heaven - ly dress, The Sav - ior came to earth; Clothed in a veil of mor - tal flesh, And bowed His head in death.

2. That aw - ful night in which be - trayed, He in - tro - duced the feast, Which we, my friends, have seen dis - played, Where each has been a guest.

3. The sol - emn scene a - bout to close, To make the whole com - plete, He meek - ly from com - mun - ion rose And washed His ser - vants' feet.

4. "To each," He said, "Let oth - ers do As I, your Lord, have done: The heaven - ly pat - tern still pur - sue, In form as I have shown."

5. Since Christ has the ex - am - ple set, Re - cord - ed in His Word: We'll hum - bly wash each oth - er's feet, O - bed - ient to our Lord.

from *Zion's Hymns*, 1854
C.M.

Hugh Wilson, c. 1800
MARTYRDOM

WHY THE LORD'S SUPPER AND FEET WASHING GO TOGETHER

Chapter Six

CHAPTER SIX

In this last chapter I will summarize why I think the Lord's Supper and feet washing go together, why I subscribe to the traditional Free Will Baptist belief in feet washing "in connection with the Lord's Supper." This question intersects with the ritual and symbolic nature of the washing of the saints' feet as it relates to the Lord's Supper—what sort of ritual are these ceremonies, and what do they symbolize?[1]

RITUAL AND NON-RITUAL ORDINANCES

Practices ordained by God may or may not be ritual in nature. An inductive examination of the Bible shows that one can subdivide New Covenant ordinances into two categories: ritual ordinances and non-ritual ordinances. Ritual ordinances include practices such as baptism, laying on of hands, the Lord's Supper, feet washing, and anointing the sick with oil. Non-ritual ordinances include such practices as corporate worship, the public ministry of the Word, prayer, fasting, singing, almsgiving, and so forth.

INITIATORY, OCCASIONAL, AND REGULAR RITUAL ORDINANCES

An inductive investigation of the New Testament also indicates that one can subdivide ritual ordinances into three groups: *initiatory* ritual ordinances, *regular* ritual ordinances, and *occasional* ritual ordinances. Baptism is universally acknowledged as the initiatory ritual ordinance of the church. (Free Will Baptists traditionally included laying on of hands after baptism to symbolize the reception of the Holy Spirit as part of the initiatory ritual of the church—Hebrews 6:2; Acts 8:17, 18). All traditions—except Quakers, who don't believe in any of it—acknowledge that baptism is the initiatory ritual of the church. Then there are occasional ritual ordinances, such as anointing the sick with oil, demanded by the occasion. In the middle category are regular ritual ordinances. Every Protestant will admit that the Lord's Supper is a regular ritual ordinance of the church. But some would wish to place feet washing in the category of occasional ritual ordinances. We have to ask the question, is the washing of the saints' feet a regular or an occasional ritual ordinance? Many mainline Protestant churches, as well as the Eastern Orthodox and Catholic churches, have in their worship or prayer books an official liturgical rite for the literal ritual observance of feet washing. But they see it as an occasional ritual ordinance, not a regular one.

NON-RITUAL ORDINANCES	RITUAL ORDINANCES		
	INITIATORY	REGULAR	OCCASIONAL
Corporate worship, public ministry of the Word, prayer, fasting, singing, almsgiving, etc.	Baptism	Lord's Supper Feet Washing	Anointing with Oil

THE MEANING OF BAPTISM, THE INITIATORY RITUAL ORDINANCE

In the initiatory ritual ordinance of baptism, the believer memorializes two things: (1) Christ's death and resurrection (buried with Christ, raised to newness of life) and (2) his own participation in Christ's death and resurrection through faith—his own death to sin and resurrection to newness of life. Leroy Forlines, as I mentioned in chapter four, has masterfully shown us that death to sin in Romans 6, that strong baptismal passage, refers to atonement and justification—the objective work of Christ in our lives. Being raised to newness of life in the same passage refers to sanctification—the subjective work of Christ in our lives that necessarily follows from the objective work.[2]

> Therefore we are buried with him by baptism into death: that like as Christ was raised up from the dead by the glory of the Father, even so we also should walk in newness of life. For if we have been planted together in the likeness of his death, we shall be also in the likeness of his resurrection: Knowing this, that our old man is crucified with him, that the body of sin might be destroyed, that henceforth we should not serve sin (Romans 6:4-6, KJV).

So we see in baptism a pictorial or symbolic ritual that illustrates for us the objective and subjective aspects of the work of Christ. Christ's death and resurrection, our death to sin and resurrection to newness of life—that is what baptism symbolizes.

THE MEANING OF THE LORD'S SUPPER

Protestant theologians agree that the Lord's Supper is a regular ritual ordinance that, among other things, reminds us of what our baptism was all about. Especially when one looks into the more liturgical segments of Protestantism, there is much discussion about confirming in our minds and remembering our baptism when we come to the Eucharist or the Lord's Supper.[3]

This presents us with a great problem, however. The initiatory ritual ordinance of baptism symbolizes the objective and subjective aspects of our union with Christ, Christ's death and resurrection, our death to sin and resurrection to newness of life, our justification and sanctification. It's inconceivable that the only *regular* ritual ordinance of the church with which to commemorate what Christ has done for us is the Lord's Supper because this represents an incomplete picture of our redemption in Christ. Yet, if the Lord's Supper is the only regular ritual ordinance of the church, then that is the result. The Lord's Supper represents the objective aspects of the work of Christ for us: His death, our death to sin, our justification. To observe only the Lord's Supper in the life of the church presents an imbalanced picture of Christ's work for us and in us, and our life in Him. Indeed, it presents only half the gospel.[4]

CORRECTING THE DICHOTOMY

The traditional Free Will Baptist understanding of feet washing in connection with the Lord's Supper corrects this dichotomized presentation of our redemption in Christ and its meaning. It's no accident or coincidence in my judgment. Baptism pictorially symbolizes

- Christ's death *and* resurrection.
- death to sin *and* resurrection to newness of life.
- justification *and* sanctification.
- the objective *and* subjective aspects of our union with Christ.

In short, baptism symbolizes the life, death, and resurrection of Christ and their redemptive significance for us. That is the gospel. Yet the Lord's Supper—by itself—represents *only* Christ's death, our death to sin, justification, the objective aspects of our union with Christ. It does not symbolize the gospel in its entirety.

TWO REGULAR RITUAL ORDINANCES

To symbolize *meaningfully and completely* the redemptive significance of Christ's life, death, and resurrection and not exclude its radical, life-changing efficacy in our subjective experience, the church must observe two regular ritual ordinances. The Lord's Supper, by itself, will not do it. Again, I do not think it was coincidental that Christ commanded the washing of the saints' feet in connection with the Lord's Supper. Only by having the Supper and the feet washing together can we symbolize our wondrous redemption in the corporate life of the church.

Thus, as I said in chapter two, Free Will Baptists believe in a two-pronged gospel, and so we believe in a two-pronged communion. In the first prong of communion, the Lord's Supper, we celebrate what God in Christ has done *for us*:

- Christ's death
- our death in Him
- justification
- Christ's work for us
- the first great commandment
- us and Christ
- the objective
- the vertical (our relationship upward, to God)

In the second prong, feet washing, we celebrate the *effects* in our everyday lives of what God in Christ has done for us—what He is doing *in us*:

- Christ's resurrection
- our resurrection to newness of life

85

- sanctification

- Christ's work in us

- the second great commandment

- us and others

- the subjective

- the horizontal (our relationship outward, to others)

SYMBOLISM OF THE LORD'S SUPPER AND FEET WASHING

THE LORD'S SUPPER	FEET WASHING
Christ's death	Christ's resurrection
our death in Him	our resurrection to newness of life
justification	sanctification
Christ's work for us	Christ's work in us
the first great commandment	the second great commandment
us and Christ	us and others
the objective	the subjective
the vertical	the horizontal

So the Lord's Supper and feet washing are complementary. Like love and marriage, "you can't have one without the other." Or at least having one without the other is incoherent and presents an incomplete picture of our redemption in Christ. Just as Jesus Christ has left the church with an initiatory ritual ordinance that symbolizes His full-orbed gospel, so He has left us with two regular ritual ordinances that, together, symbolize that gospel.

By observing feet washing, we realize in the church's corporate life and worship that salvation is not just objective reconciliation with God through the death of Christ ("me and Jesus, we got our own thing going"). We ritually demonstrate that this reconciliation brings us into a new kind of life subjectively—resurrection life that issues forth in sanctification and breaks out into a radically new way of being reconciled to others through Jesus Christ. Only by observing both the Lord's Supper and the washing of the saints' feet can we meaningfully—and scripturally—symbolize the whole gospel in the worship of the church.

NOTES

1. Some people who object to feet washing feel the need to establish that feet washing is not "equivalent to" or "on the same level as" or "as important as" baptism and the Lord's Supper. It is as though a practice must meet those criteria to be considered an ordinance. When people ask me, "You don't think feet washing is as important as baptism or the Lord's Supper, do you?" I simply say that is not an appropriate question. God has provided His people practices for their gracious edification, and He wants them to observe those practices. The New Testament does not give us details about which ones are more or less important. Is public prayer more important than public reading of Scripture? Is singing praise to God more important than church discipline? Is the ordination of pastors more important than preaching? Is baptism more important than the Lord's Supper? Is the Lord's Supper more important than preaching? How could we possibly know the answer to these questions from reading the New Testament? Again, these are not questions that the New Testament *leads* us to ask. God simply gives us ordinances that we are to observe, and He expects us to obey. Is baptism more "important" than the Lord's Supper? I don't know. I suppose one could argue that in some ways it is more primary. Yet I don't think it is a question the Scriptures lead us to ask. I don't think the New Testament gives us warrant to establish a hierarchy of importance of God's ordinances. It simply says we ought to observe them (See chapter two for my definition of ordinances).

2. See Forlines, 146-58.

3. An example of this is found in the United Methodist publication *By Water and Spirit: A United Methodist Understanding of Baptism*: "In celebrating the Eucharist, we remember the grace given to us in our baptism and partake of the spiritual food necessary for sustaining and fulfilling the promises of salvation. Because the table at which we gather belongs to the Lord, it should be open to all who respond to Christ's love, regardless of age or church membership. The Wesleyan tradition has always recognized that Holy Communion may be an occasion for the reception of converting, justifying, and sanctifying grace. Unbaptized persons who receive communion should be counseled and nurtured toward baptism as soon as possible." (http://www.gbod.org/worship/articles/water_spirit/baptism.html#Anchor1)

4. I am not arguing that the Lord's Supper does not express the unity and fellowship of the church (1 Corinthians 10:17). Yet it is a minor aspect of the Supper, as evidenced by the fact that theologians usually write only a sentence or two about this aspect of the Lord's Supper, as compared with many pages on the rite's symbolism of Christ's death. My

argument centers on what the Lord's Supper symbolizes: the broken body and shed blood of Christ in His atoning, justifying death. Thus, I agree with what the nineteenth-century Baptist author James M. Pendleton wrote: "Some will perhaps say that in the Lord's Supper we express our Christian fellowship for our fellow-communicants. This is done only in an indirect and incidental manner. Our communion, according to the teaching of Paul, is the communion of the body and the blood of Christ. It is a solemn celebration of his atoning death." (James M. Pendleton, *Christian Doctrines: A Compendium of Theology* [Valley Forge, Penn.: Judson, {1878}, repr. 1976].)

FEET WASHING

1. I want to be like Je-sus, His word my soul to keep And
2. Ye call me Lord and Mas-ter, "Well done!" for so I am And
3. If I, your Lord and Mas-ter, And now have washed your feet; That
4. I gave you this ex-am-ple, That you, my will re-plete; To

hum-bly, like Him kneel-ing, and wash my broth-er's feet.
giv'n you this ex-am-ple, to do as I com-mand
all who fol-low af-ter, this ser-vice to re-peat.
fol-low this com-mand-ment, and wash each oth-er's feet.

Dear Lord may I be a lit-tle more hum-ble, Dai-ly fol-low

Dear Lord may I show just a lit-tle more love,

Thee, may I not re-treat. Ere I should cause my bro-ther to

Dai-ly follow Thee, may I not re-treat. may I not re-treat Ere I should cause my broth-er to

stum-ble May I hum-bly kneel and wash His feet.

stum-ble far from heav-en's Dove May I hum-bly kneel and wash His feet wash my broth-er's feet.

R. E. Smallwood
© 1938 R. E. Smallwood
7.6.7.6. with refrain

R. E. Smallwood
Arranged by N. P. Gates/James M. Stevens
FEET WASHING

89

APPENDIX ONE

HISTORICAL REFLECTIONS ON ORDINANCES AND SACRAMENTS

SACRAMENTS AND SACRAMENTALISM

To understand better how to think about ordinances, it is helpful to look briefly at the treatment of sacraments and ordinances in the history of Christian thought. The medieval Roman Catholic and early Reformation (Protestant) views of the sacraments are important to understand. A knowledge of these views not only helps one see the historical and theological contexts out of which Baptist understandings of ordinances arose. It also helps one understand why Reformation views of the sacraments predisposed the Reformers to define sacraments the way they did.

The Christian fathers did not define, enumerate, or classify sacraments or ordinances. Indeed, the question of ordinances and sacraments did not arise until much later in the history of Christianity. Tertullian (c. 160-c. 220) was the first Christian thinker to employ the Latin term *sacramentum*, but he used it to discuss countless sacred ceremonies.[1] "The same loose usage is found in the writings of Augustine, Hilary, Leo the Great, Gregory the Great, and others."[2] Augustine (354-430), though he did not strictly define "sacrament," was the first theologian to use the term in a way similar to its present use. He described a sacrament as a "visible sign of an invisible grace." [3]

The concept of sacrament did not take shape until the end of the seventh century. Yet Augustine had set into motion the central medieval Catholic notion of the sacraments: that they convey divine grace. An example of this doctrine is found in Peter Lombard (c. 1100-1160), who fixed the number of the sacraments at seven.[4]

Lombard taught that "God instituted the remedies of sacraments against the wounds of original and actual sin. . . . Sacraments were instituted, therefore, for the sake, not only of signifying [symbolizing] but also of sanctifying."[5] Thomas Aquinas (1225-1274) defined a sacrament as "a sign of a sacred thing, since it is a means of sanctifying men."[6] Gabriel Biel (c. 1415-1495), the foremost theologian against whom Martin Luther reacted, insisted that, though people may obtain *gratia gratis data* (grace freely given) without the sacraments, they must partake of the sacraments to receive the *gratia gratum faciens* (the grace that makes one a friend of God)—that is, saving grace.[7]

The view that the sacraments transmit divine grace contributed to the theological context of the Protestant Reformation. The Magisterial Reformers (and their followers, Lutherans, Calvinists, and Anglicans) reacted strongly against five of the seven sacraments. Of these five, the most dangerous was penance, since it reinforced the medieval notion that God rewarded good works (merit) with saving grace. Yet, while the major Protestant Reformers rejected five of the seven sacraments, they still held to a basic sacramentalism. They believed that the sacraments of baptism and the Lord's Supper convey divine grace. Martin Luther (1483-1546), John Calvin (1509-1564), and the English Reformers (Anglicans) believed that the sacraments have a special, saving effect on the partaker. This is borne out in Luther and Calvin's disagreement with Zwingli and the Anabaptists, who held that the sacraments were merely symbolic and nothing more.

Luther made his views clear in such statements as the following from his *Short Catechism* (1529):

> What is the Sacrament of the Altar? *Answer.* It is the very Body and Blood of our Lord Jesus Christ, under

the Bread and Wine, for us Christians to eat and to drink. . . .What avails us to eat and drink thus? Answer. This is shown us by the words which stand there, *"Given for you and shed for you for the remission of sins."* That is to say, that in the Sacrament forgiveness of sins, life, and salvation are bestowed on us by these words.[8]

Luther held the views of Duns Scotus and other medieval thinkers that the sacraments were *efficacia signa* (efficacious signs) of divine grace.[9]

Calvin and his followers were less sacramentalistic than Luther. Yet they still insisted that special grace is present when a faithful partaker receives the sacraments (or an infant of at least one faithful parent receives baptism). In his *Short Treatise on the Holy Supper of Our Lord Jesus Christ*, Calvin stated that, in the Supper, "the Lord displays to us all the treasures of his spiritual grace, inasmuch as he associates us in all the blessings and riches of our Lord Jesus. . . . It is indeed true that this same grace is offered us by the gospel, yet as in the Supper we have more ample certainty, and fuller enjoyment of it, with good cause do we recognise this fruit as coming from it."[10] The framers of the *Westminster Shorter Catechism*, followers of Calvin, stated that "a sacrament is a holy ordinance instituted by Christ, wherein, by sensible signs, Christ, and the benefits of the new covenant, are represented, sealed, and applied to believers."[11]

The *Thirty-Nine Articles* of the Reformation Church of England are even more direct about the nature of sacraments as conveyers of grace: "Sacraments ordained of Christ be not only badges or tokens of Christian men's profession, but rather they be certain sure witnesses, and effectual signs of grace, and God's good will toward us, by the which he doth work invisibly in us, and doth not only quicken, but also strengthen and confirm our Faith in him."[12]

With the exception of the Anabaptists and Baptists, most early Protestants (Lutherans, Reformed, Anglican) believed that the sacraments, in some way or another, conveyed divine grace.[13] Thus they preferred the accepted term *sacrament* to the term *ordinance*, which was increasingly used by the Anabaptists and their kin.

ORDINANCES

The Anabaptists wished to cut away the encumbrances of Roman Catholic tradition and follow the pattern of the New Testament churches. In this desire they differed in important ways from the Lutherans, Calvinists, and Anglicans. Their "biblicism" or "restorationism" manifested itself in such doctrines as believer's baptism, the church as a gathered community of believers rather than a state church (institutional separation of church and state), and complete freedom of conscience. This biblicism also affected the Anabaptists' conception of ordinances.[14] The Anabaptists wholly rejected sacramentalism. The ordinances, far from conveying divine grace, were symbols or pictures that memorialize Christ and His gospel. This mindset appears in *The Dordrecht Confession*, the most influential of the early Anabaptist/Mennonite confessions of faith. In this confession the Lord's Supper is said to be "in *commemoration* of the death and sufferings of the Lord . . . to *remind* us of the benefit of the said death and sufferings of Christ." Feet washing is described as "a sign to *remind* us of the true washing—the washing and purification of the soul in the blood of Christ."[15] The Anabaptists rejected sacramentalism and simply affirmed that ordinances are sacred rites ordained by God. Thus, they freed themselves from any preconceived notion of sacraments—whether Catholic or Protestant, whether seven or two.

The number of ordinances varies from one Anabaptist author to another. For example, Dirk Phillips, a prominent sixteenth-century

Anabaptist, listed "the foot washing of the saints" as one of seven Christian ordinances.[16] Some Anabaptists emphasized certain rituals more than others, but they did not define and enumerate sacraments the way the church in the Middle Ages had. In their quest to imitate the simplicity of the primitive church, they merely wanted to reenact those rituals that were enacted in the New Testament. This holds true for American Mennonites today. For example, a widely used Mennonite confession published by a major Mennonite publisher affirms six ordinances: baptism, the Lord's Supper, feet washing, women's head covering, the kiss of charity, and anointing with oil.[17]

Our Free Will Baptist forebears, the General Baptists, arose in England in the early seventeenth century. Their doctrine of the church was influenced by the Mennonites. They shared the Anabaptist aversion to sacramentalism and tended toward a biblicist view of ordinances. While in those early days disagreements arose on just which rites were ordinances, the General Baptists maintained a much more open-ended definition of ordinances than did their Particular Baptist brethren, who originated a generation later.

The Particular Baptists, who arose out of the Calvinist Independents (Congregationalists) in England, modeled their *Second London Confession of Faith* after the Calvinistic *Westminster Confession of Faith*. In their views many Particular Baptists straddled the fence between an Anabaptist (symbolic, memorial) view of the ordinances and a more Calvinistic view. This is evidenced by chapter 30, "Of the Lord's Supper," in the *Second London Confession*. This chapter affirms the presence of Christ in the elements of the Lord's Supper: "Worthy receivers, outwardly partaking of the visible Elements in this Ordinance, do then also inwardly by faith, really and indeed, yet not carnally, and corporally, but spiritually receive, and feed upon Christ crucified & all the benefits of his death."[18] This article repeats the *Westminster Confession of Faith* verbatim, except that it uses the word *ordinance* instead of *sacrament*. The Calvinist Baptists owed more to the teaching of Calvin and the early Reformed tradition on the nature of the ordinances than the General Baptists did.

SOME CONCLUSIONS AND IMPLICATIONS

What conclusions should we draw from this historical sketch? First, we must recognize the silence of the early Christian fathers on this subject. Not until Tertullian was the term *sacramentum* employed. Then it was used to describe all manner of Christian ceremonies and rituals that were taught by Christ and the apostles. Thus, the Christian fathers spoke in a more general way about various and sundry rituals to be practiced in the churches (though some emphasized or practiced certain rituals more or less than others). They did not delineate a set number of sacraments.[19] It is also clear that the concept of "sacrament" as a means of divine grace did not gain currency until Augustine, and then only in seed form. Not until the seventh century did this conception crystallize. Second, we must understand that the essential medieval Catholic conception of sacraments was that they convey divine grace.

Third, the Reformers, in their reaction against Catholic dogma, did not reject sacramentalism. They only modified it. This modification predisposed Luther and Calvin to reject feet washing as a sacrament. Their view of sacraments was *synthetic*. They were synthesizing the medieval sacramental tradition rather than dispensing with it, and thus were unable to free themselves from the basic sacramental theology of the medieval church. The difference between Roman Catholic sacraments and Protestant sacraments was one of degree, not of kind. In other words, the debate was not over whether the sacraments convey grace, but what degree of grace, and whether faith is necessary for the reception of sacramental grace. Yet there was no disagreement that, in the sacraments, God sovereignly conveys His grace.

This synthetic view of sacraments caused the Reformers to work within the accepted number of sacraments (seven) and decide which ones to keep and which ones to throw out, rather than scrapping the whole medieval sacramental system and starting from scratch. Thus, the Reformers limited the sacraments to two: baptism and the Lord's Supper. They were unable to get past centuries of theological growth. Consequently, they were unable to conceive of sacraments outside of the Catholic seven. Furthermore, it was difficult for them to conceive of God conveying grace through any of the other five Catholic sacraments (marriage, extreme unction, ordination, confirmation, and penance).

It is probable, then, that the Reformers' synthetic view of the sacraments predisposed them not to view feet washing (or anything else) as a sacrament. It would not have made sense to them that something like feet washing could be a means of grace. This notion grew out of the idea that God *sovereignly* conveys His grace through the sacraments. It is easy to understand how God could be seen as sovereignly "acting upon" the passive recipient in baptism or the Lord's Supper. It is not so easy to see how God could do the same in the washing of the saints' feet. Thus, the Reformers discounted feet washing of necessity because it failed to measure up to their definition of sacraments. Additionally, Luther preached against feet washing, using a widely held early Protestant view: Christians should avoid feet washing because of the pomp, circumstance, and pride evident when the pope washed the feet of twelve of his cardinals every Maundy Thursday (the Thursday before Easter).[20] First, since the pope does it, it must be bad. Second, Luther argued, it is a show of pride and not of humility. To summarize, the Reformers were predisposed to reject feet washing as a sacrament because it failed to meet their criteria of a sacrament: that it is a ritual in which God acts upon faithful recipients, sovereignly conveying His grace upon them.

The reason Anabaptists were predisposed to include feet washing and other rites as Christian ordinances was precisely the opposite. Their biblicism forced them to go back to the New Testament for instructions and patterns for the practices of the church. This, in turn, opened them up to a radically different way of conceptualizing sacraments or ordinances. They began to see ordinances as rites that God *ordained*, nothing more, nothing less. These same attitudes opened the seventeenth-century Baptists to an understanding of the ordinances that was not straitjacketed by medieval notions.

Additionally, the Anabaptists and General Baptists rejected the idea that the sacraments convey divine grace. It was much more natural for them to view a rite like feet washing as an ordinance, since they rejected the criterion that sacraments convey divine grace. The Particular Baptists, however, limited the ordinances to baptism and the Lord's Supper, perhaps because their view of ordinances was an amalgamation of the sacrament-theology of the Calvinists and the ordinance-theology of the Anabaptists.

NOTES

1. J. N. D. Kelley, *Early Christian Doctrines* (London: A & C Black, 1977), 193; David R. Plaster, *Ordinances: What Are They?* (Winona Lake, Ind.: BMH, 1985), 16.

2. Louis Berkhof, *The History of Christian Doctrines* (Grand Rapids: Eerdmans, 1937), 242.

3. Plaster, 16.

4. Baptism, confirmation, the Lord's Supper, penance, extreme unction, ordination, and marriage. It is interesting to note that, in Roman Catholicism, feet washing was viewed as a "sacramental," though not a full-fledged sacrament. *The Catholic Encyclopedia* states: "The action of Christ after the Last Supper (John, xiii, 1-15) must also have invested [the

washing of feet] with a deep religious significance, and in fact down to the time of St. Bernard we find ecclesiastical writers, at least occasionally, applying to this ceremony the term *Sacramentum* in its wider sense, by which they no doubt meant that it possessed the virtue of what we now call a sacramental. Christ's command to wash one another's feet must have been understood from the beginning in a literal sense, for St. Paul (I Tim., v, 10) implies that a widow to be honored and consecrated in the Church should be one 'having testimony for her good works, if she have received to harbour, if she have washed the saints' feet'. This tradition, we may believe, has never been interrupted. . . ." *The Catholic Encyclopedia* (New York: Encyclopedia Press, 1913), s.v. "Washing of Feet and Hands," by Herbert Thurston.

5. Peter Lombard, *The Four Books of Sentences* (book 4, distinction 1, chapters 1 and 4) in Eugene R. Fairweather, ed., *A Scholastic Miscellany: Anselm to Ockham* (Philadelphia: Westminster, 1951), 338-39.

6. Cited in Reinhold Seeberg, *Text-book of the History of Doctrines*, vol. 2, trans. Charles E. Hay (Philadelphia: Lutheran Publication Society, 1905), 125.

7. Heiko A. Oberman, *The Harvest of Medieval Theology: Gabriel Biel and Late Medieval Nominalism* (Cambridge: Harvard University Press, 1963), 135-40.

8. Martin Luther, "The Short Catechism, 1529," in Henry Bettenson, ed., *Documents of the Christian Church* (New York: Oxford University Press, 1947), 293-94.

9. Seeberg, 282. It must be stressed here that Luther was vehemently opposed to transubstantiation—the view that the substance of the bread and wine literally *became* the body and blood of Christ—and the Lord's Supper as a sacrifice. Yet it is clear that Luther still believed that special grace was bestowed on the believing partaker of the Supper.

10. John Calvin, *Short Treatise on the Holy Supper of Our Lord Jesus Christ*, in John Dillenberger, ed., *John Calvin: Selections from His Writings* (n.p.: Scholars Press, 1975), 512.

11. *The Westminster Shorter Catechism*, question 92, in *The Book of Confessions* (New York: The General Assembly of the Presbyterian Church U.S.A., 1983.)

12. From "Articles of Religion," article 25, in *The Book of Common Prayer* (New York: James Pott and Company, 1892), 652.

13. Huldrych Zwingli (1484-1531) is an exception to this general rule. His followers either became Anabaptists or eventually merged with the Calvinists. See W. P. Stephens, *The Theology of Huldrych Zwingli* (Oxford: Oxford University Press, 1986), 180-93.

14. Though some early Anabaptist writers used the word *sacrament, ordinance* eventually became the norm, being more in line with the theology of the Anabaptists.

15. *The Dordrecht Confession*, in William L. Lumpkin, ed., *Baptist Confessions of Faith* (Valley Forge, Penn.: Judson, 1959), 73-74. (Italics added.)

16. Timothy George, *Theology of the Reformers* (Nashville: Broadman, 1988), 294. Used by permission.

17. *Mennonites: Who They Are, What They Believe* (Harrisonburg, Virginia: Christian Light Publications, n.d.). This is the statement of faith printed in the catalog of Christian Light Publications. For a similar list, see Daniel Kauffman, ed. *Doctrines of the Bible* (Scottdale, Penn.: Herald, 1928), 381. Brethren and Grace Brethren are another example; they practice four ordinances: baptism, the Lord's Supper, feet washing, and the love feast (*agape* meal).

18. *The Second London Confession*, in Lumpkin, 293. See also Samuel Waldron, *A Modern Exposition of the 1689 Baptist Confession of Faith* (Durham, England: Evangelical Press, 1989), 360-74.

19. Anglican scholar Stephen W. Sykes, discussing the number of the sacraments, offers the following insight: "Modern theology has come to think that the reasons that led Roman Catholics and Protestants to be so certain and vehement in their rival enumerations are far from cogent. On the other hand, the church developed in the course of its history a very large number of rituals. . . ." Stephen W. Sykes, "The Sacraments," in *Christian Theology: An Introduction to Its Traditions and Tasks*, Peter C. Hodgson and Robert H. King, eds. (Philadelphia: Fortress, 1982), 274. Cf. John Macquarrie, "Baptism, Confirmation, Eucharist," in *Signs of Faith, Hope, and Love: The Christian Sacraments Today* (San Francisco: Collins Liturgical, 1988), 58.

20. It is ironic that present-day Lutherans, in both the ELCA and the Missouri Synod, encourage the practice of feet washing on Maundy Thursday. See, e.g., Jay C. Rochelle, "Improve Your Serve: Foot Washing Jars Us Out of Complacency," *The Lutheran Magazine* (April 1996), 10-12. The *Lutheran Book of Worship* contains instructions for feet washing. (Washing feet on Maundy Thursday became popular in the seventh century. The word *maundy* is tied directly to the feet washing command in John 13. Its Latin root is *mandatum*, which means "commandment.")

APPENDIX TWO

AUGUSTINE ON JOHN 13[1]

Knowing, then, these things, "He riseth from Supper, and layeth aside His garments; and took a towel, and girded Himself. After that He poureth water into a basin, and began to wash the disciples' feet, and to wipe them with the towel wherewith He was girded." We ought, dearly beloved, carefully to mark the meaning of the evangelist; because that, when about to speak of the pre-eminent humility of the Lord, it was his desire first to commend His majesty. It is in reference to this that He says, "Jesus knowing that the Father had given all things into His hands, and that He has come from God, and is going to God." It is He, therefore, into whose hands the Father had given all things, who now washes, not the disciples' hands, but their feet: and it was just while knowing that He had come from God, and was proceeding to God, that He discharged the office of a servant, not of God the Lord, but of man. And this also is referred to by the prefatory notice He has been pleased to make of His betrayer, who was now come as such, and was not unknown to Him; that the greatness of His humility should be still further enhanced by the fact that He did not esteem it beneath His dignity to wash also the feet of one whose hands He already foresaw to be steeped in wickedness.

But why should we wonder that He rose from Supper, and laid aside His garments, who, being in the form of God, made Himself of no reputation?[2] And why should we wonder, if He girded Himself with a towel, who took upon Him the form of a servant, and was found in the likeness of a man? (Phil. 2:6, 7). Why wonder, if He poured water into a basin wherewith to wash His disciples' feet, who poured His blood upon the earth to wash away the filth of their sins? Why wonder, if with the towel wherewith He was girded He wiped the feet He had washed, who with the very flesh that clothed Him laid a firm pathway for the footsteps of His evangelists? In order, indeed, to gird Himself with the towel, He laid aside the garments He wore; but when He emptied Himself [of His divine glory] in order to assume the form of a servant, He laid not down what He had, but assumed that which He had not before. When about to be crucified, He was indeed stripped of His garments, and when dead was wrapped in linen clothes: and all that suffering of His is our purification. When, therefore, about to suffer the last extremities [of humiliation,] He here illustrated beforehand its friendly compliances; not only to those for whom He was about to endure death, but to him also who had resolved on betraying Him to death. Because so great is the beneficence of human humility, that even the Divine Majesty was pleased to commend it by His own example; for proud man would have perished eternally, had he not been found by the lowly God. For the Son of man came to seek and to save that which was lost (Luke 19:10). And as he was lost by imitating the pride of the deceiver, let him now, when found, imitate the Redeemer's humility.

* * * * *

When the Lord was washing the disciples' feet, "He cometh to Simon Peter; and Peter saith unto Him, Lord, dost Thou wash my feet?" For who would not be filled with fear at having his feet washed by the Son of God? Although, therefore, it was a piece of the greatest audacity for the servant to contradict his Lord, the creature his God; yet Peter preferred doing this to the suffering of his feet to be washed by his Lord and God. Nor ought we to think that Peter was one amongst others who so expressed their fear and refusal, seeing that others before him had suffered it to be done to themselves with cheerfulness and equanimity. For it is easier so to understand the words of the Gospel, because that, after saying, "He began to wash the disciples' feet, and to wipe them with the towel wherewith He was girded," it is then added, "Then cometh He to Simon Peter," as if He had already washed the feet of some, and after them had now come to the first of them all. For who can fail to know that the most blessed Peter was the first of the apostles? But we are not so to understand it, that it was after some others that He came to him; but that He began with him.[3] When, therefore, He began to wash the disciples' feet, He came to him with whom He began, namely, to Peter; and then Peter took fright at what any one of them might have been frightened, and said, "Lord, dost thou wash my feet?" What is implied in this "thou"? and what in "my"? These are subjects for thought rather than for speech; lest perchance any adequate conception the soul may have formed of such words may fail of explanation in the utterance.

But "Jesus answered and said unto him, What I do thou knowest not now, but thou shalt know hereafter." And not even yet, terrified as he was by the sublimity of the Lord's action, does he allow it to be done, while ignorant of its purpose; but is unwilling to see, unable to endure, that Christ should thus humble Himself to his very feet. "Thou shalt never," he says, "wash my feet." What is this "never" [*in aeternum*]? I will never endure, never suffer, never permit it: that is, a thing is not done "*in aeternum*" which is never done. Then the Saviour, to terrify His reluctant patient with the danger of his own salvation, says, "If I wash thee not, thou hast no part with me." He speaks in this way, "If I wash thee not," when He was referring only to his feet; just as it is customary to say, You are trampling on me, when it is only the foot that is trampled on. And now the other, in a perturbation of love and fear, and more frightened at the thought that Christ should be withheld from him, than even to see Him humbled at his feet, exclaims, "Lord, not my feet only, but also my hands and my head." Since this, indeed, is Thy threat, that my bodily members must be washed by Thee, not only do I no longer withhold the lowest, but I lay the foremost also at Thy disposal. Deny me not having a part with Thee, and I deny Thee not any part of my body to be washed.

"Jesus saith to him, He that is washed needeth not save to wash his feet, but is clean every whit." Some one perhaps may be aroused at this, and say: Nay, but if he is every whit clean, what need has He even to wash his feet? But the Lord knew what He was saying, even though our weakness reach not into His secret purposes. Nevertheless, so far as He is pleased to instruct and teach us out of His law, up to the little measure of my apprehension, I would also, with His help, make some answer bearing on the depths of this question: and, first of all, I shall have no difficulty in showing that there is no self-contradiction in the manner of expression. For who may not say, as here, with the greatest propriety, He is all clean, except[4] his feet?—although he would speak with greater elegance were he to say, He is all clean, save[5] his feet; which is equivalent in meaning. Thus, then, doth the Lord say, "He needeth not save to wash his feet, but is all clean." All, that is, except, or save[6] his feet, which he still needs to wash.

But what is this? what does it mean? and what is there in it we need to examine? The Lord says, The Truth declares that even he who has been washed has need still to wash his feet. What, my brethren, what think you of it, save that in holy baptism a man has all of him washed, not all save his feet, but every whit; and yet, while thereafter living in this human state, he cannot fail to tread on the ground with his feet. And thus our human feelings themselves, which are inseparable from our mortal life on earth, are like feet wherewith we are brought into sensible contact with human affairs; and are so in such a way, that if we say we have no sin, we deceive ourselves, and the truth is not in us (1 John 1:8). And every day, therefore, is He who intercedeth for us (Rom. 8:34), washing our feet: and that we, too, have daily need to be washing our feet, that is ordering aright the path of our spiritual footsteps, we acknowledge even in the Lord's prayer, when we say, "Forgive us our debts as we forgive our debtors" (Matthew 6:12). For "if," as it is written, "we confess our sins," then verily is He, who washed His disciples' feet, "faithful and just to forgive us our sins, and to cleanse us from all unrighteousness" (1 John 1:9), that is, even to our feet wherewith we walk on the earth.

Accordingly the Church, which Christ cleanseth with the washing of water in the word, is without spot and wrinkle (Ephe. 5:26–27), not only in the case of those who are taken away immediately after the washing of regeneration from the contagious influence of this life, and tread not the earth so as to make necessary the washing of their feet, but in those also who have experienced such mercy from the Lord as to be enabled to quit this present life even with feet that have been washed. But although the Church be also clean in respect of those who tarry on earth, because they live righteously; yet have they need to be washing their feet, because they assuredly are not without sin. For this cause is it said in the Song of Songs, "I have washed my feet; how shall I defile them?" (Song of Solo. 5:3). For one so speaks when he is constrained to come to Christ, and in coming has to bring his feet into contact with the ground. But again, there is another question that arises. Is not Christ above? Hath He not ascended into heaven, and sitteth He not at the Father's right hand? Does not the apostle expressly declare, "If ye then be risen with Christ, seek those things which are above, where Christ sitteth on the right hand of God. Set your affection on things above, not on things on the earth"? (Colossians 3:1, 2). How is it, then, that to get to Christ we are compelled to tread the earth, since rather our hearts ought to be turned upwards toward the Lord, that we may be enabled to dwell in His presence? You see, brethren, the shortness of the time to-day curtails our consideration of this question. And if you perhaps fail in some measure to do so, yet I for my part see how much clearing up it requires. And therefore I beg of you to suffer it rather to be adjourned, than to be treated now in too negligent and restricted a manner; and your expectations will not be defrauded, but only deferred. For the Lord who thus makes us your debtors, will be present to enable us also to pay our debts.

* * * * *

. . . The topic on which we were speaking, and which led to our entering on this inquiry, was our Lord's washing His disciples' feet, after the disciples themselves had already been washed, and needed not, save to wash their feet. And we there saw it to be understood that a man is indeed wholly washed in baptism; but while thereafter he liveth in this present world, and with the feet of his human passions treadeth on this earth, that is, in his life-intercourse with others, he contracts enough to call forth the prayer, "Forgive us our debts" (Matt. 6:12). And, thus, from these also is he cleansed by Him who washed His disciples' feet (John 13:5), and ceaseth not to make intercession for us (Rom. 8:34). And here occurred the words of the Church in the Song of Songs, when she saith, "I have washed my feet; how shall I defile them?" when she wished to go and open to that Being, fairer in form than the sons of men (Psalm 45:2), who had come to her and knocked, and asked her to open to Him. This gave rise to a question, which we were unwilling to compress into the narrow limits of the time, and therefore deferred till now, in what sense the Church, when on her way to Christ, may be afraid of defiling her feet, which she had washed in the baptism of Christ.

For thus she speaks: "I sleep, but my heart waketh: it is the voice of my Beloved[7] that knocketh at the gate." And then He also says: "Open to me, my sister, my nearest, my dove, my perfect one; for my head is filled with dew, and my hair with the drops of the night." And she replies: "I have put off my dress; how shall I put it on? I have washed my feet; how shall I defile them?" (Song of Solo. 5:2–3). O wonderful sacramental symbol! O lofty mystery! Does she, then, fear to defile her feet in coming to Him who washed the feet of His disciples? Her fear is genuine; for it is along the earth she has to come to Him, who is still on earth, because refusing to leave His own who are stationed here. Is it not He that saith, "Lo, I am with you always, even unto the end of the world"? (Matt. 28:20). Is it not He that saith, "Ye shall see the heavens opened, and the angels of God ascending and descending upon the Son of man"? (John 1:51). If they ascend to Him because He is above, how do they descend to Him, but because He is also here? Therefore saith the Church: "I have washed my feet; how shall I defile them?". . .

* * * * *

We have already, beloved, as the Lord was pleased to enable us, expounded to you those words of the Gospel, where the Lord, in washing His disciples' feet, says, "He that is once washed needeth not save to wash his feet, but is clean every whit." Let us now look at what follows. "And ye," He says, "are clean, but not all." And to remove the need of inquiry on our part, the evangelist has himself explained its meaning, by adding: "For He knew who it was that should betray Him; therefore said He, Ye are not all clean." Can anything be clearer? Let us therefore pass to what follows.

"So, after He had washed their feet, and had taken His garments, and was set down again, He said unto them, Know ye what I have done to you?" Now it is that the blessed Peter gets that promise fulfilled: for he had been put off when, in the midst of his trembling and asserting, "Thou shalt never wash my feet," he received the answer, "What I do, thou knowest not now, but thou shalt know hereafter" (John 13:7-8). Here, then, is that very hereafter; it is now time to tell what was a little ago deferred. Accordingly, the Lord, mindful of His foregoing promise to make him understand an act of His so unexpected, so wonderful, so frightening, and, but for His own still more terrifying rejoinder, impossible to be permitted, that the Master not only of themselves, but of angels, and the Lord not only of them, but of all things, should wash the feet of His own disciples and servants: having then promised to let him know the meaning of so important an act, when He said, "Thou shalt know afterwards," begins now to show them what it was that He did.

"Ye call me," He says, "Master and Lord: and ye say well; for so I am." "Ye say well," for ye only say the truth; I am indeed what ye say. There is a precept laid on man: "Let not thine own mouth praise thee, but the mouth of thy neighbor" (Prov. 27:2). . . .

"If I, then," He says, "your Lord and Master, have washed your feet, ye also ought to wash one another's feet. For I have given you an example, that ye should do as I have done to you." This, blessed Peter, is what thou didst not know when thou wert not allowing it to be done. This is what He promised to let thee know afterwards, when thy Master and thy Lord terrified thee into submission, and washed thy feet. We have learned, brethren, humility from the Highest; let us, as humble, do to one another what He, the Highest, did in His humility. Great is the commendation we have here of humility: and brethren do this to one another in turn, even in the visible act itself, when they treat one another with hospitality; for the practice of such humility is generally prevalent, and finds expression in the very deed that makes it discernible. And hence the apostle, when he would commend the well-deserving widow, says, "If she is hospitable, if she has washed the saints' feet" (1 Tim. 5:10). And wherever such is not the practice among the saints, what they do not with the hand they do in heart, if they are of the number of those who are addressed in the hymn of the three blessed men, "O ye holy and humble of heart, bless ye the Lord."[8] But it is far better, and beyond all dispute more accordant with the truth, that it should also be done with the hands; nor should the

Christian think it beneath him to do what was done by Christ. For when the body is bent at a brother's feet, the feeling of such humility is either awakened in the heart itself, or is strengthened if already present.

But apart from this moral understanding of the passage, we remember that the way in which we commended to your attention the grandeur of this act of the Lord's, was that, in washing the feet of disciples who were already washed and clean, the Lord instituted a sign, to the end that, on account of the human feelings that occupy us on earth, however far we may have advanced in our apprehension of righteousness, we might know that we are not exempt from sin; which He thereafter washes away by interceding for us, when we pray the Father, who is in heaven, to forgive us our debts, as we also forgive our debtors (Matt. 6:12). What connection, then, can such an understanding of the passage have with that which He afterwards gave Himself, when He explained the reason of His act in the words, "If I then, your Lord and Master, have washed your feet, ye also ought to wash one another's feet. For I have given you an example, that ye should do as I have done to you"? Can we say that even a brother may cleanse a brother from the contracted stain of wrongdoing? Yea, verily, we know that of this also we were admonished in the profound significance of this work of the Lord's, that we should confess our faults one to another, and pray for one another, even as Christ also maketh intercession for us (Rom. 8:34). Let us listen to the Apostle James, who states this precept with the greatest clearness when he says, "Confess your faults one to another, and pray one for another" (James 5:16). For of this also the Lord gave us the example. For if He who neither has, nor had, nor will have any sin, prays for our sins, how much more ought we to pray for one another's in turn! And if He forgives us, whom we have nothing to forgive; how much more ought we, who are unable to live here without sin, to forgive one another! For what else does the Lord apparently intimate in the profound significance of this sacramental sign, when He says, "For I have given you an example, that ye should do as I have done to you;" but what the apostle declares in the plainest terms, "Forgiving one another, if any man have a quarrel against any: even as Christ forgave you, so also do ye"? (Col. 3:13). Let us therefore forgive one another his faults, and pray for one another's faults, and thus in a manner be washing one another's feet. It is our part, by His grace, to be supplying the service of love and humility: it is His to hear us, and to cleanse us from all the pollution of our sins through Christ, and in Christ; so that what we forgive even to others, that is, loose on earth, may be loosed in heaven.

NOTES

1. What follows are excerpts from *Augustine's Lectures and Tractates on the Gospel According to St. John* 50-58, in Philip Schaff, ed., Nicene and Post-Nicene Fathers, Series I (Grand Rapids: Eerdmans, 1956), v. 7. Asterisks indicate transitions between tractates. Ellipses indicate transitions from one excerpt to another.

2. Literally "emptied Himself," as in the Greek.—Translator's note (hereafter,—TR.).

3. It is curious to notice how Augustin here contradicts his previous and natural explanation of the passage, in order to uphold the primacy of Peter. It looks as if here he suddenly felt that his former words were rather adverse to the notion.—TR.

4. Of course, it is a mere elegance in the Latinity to which Augustin here refers, as between *præter pedes* and *nisi pedes*, when qualifying the expression, "*Mundus est totus*" (he is all clean).—TR.

5. Of course, it is a mere elegance in the Latinity to which Augustin here refers, as between *præter pedes* and *nisi pedes*, when qualifying the expression, "*Mundus est totus*" (he is all clean).—TR.

6. Of course, it is a mere elegance in the Latinity to which Augustin here refers, as between *præter pedes* and *nisi pedes*, when qualifying the expression, "*Mundus est totus*" (he is all clean).—TR.

7. *Patruelis*, literally cousin (by the father's side).—TR.

8. Dan. 3:88; that is, in the apocryphal piece called "The Song of the Three Children," and which, as it has no place in the Hebrew Scriptures, is also omitted in our English version. Its place would fall between the 23rd and 24th verses of chap. 3.—TR.

Appendix Three
STUDY QUESTIONS

(These questions are also available in a downloadable format at www.RandallHouse.com.)

CHAPTER ONE

"Introductory Reflections on Feet Washing"

1. Name some Christian denominations that practice feet washing. Were you surprised that so many do?

2. Is the practice of feet washing of recent origin among Free Will Baptists? Is it limited to certain regions of the United States? What are the implications of this for our current practice?

3. Discuss the meaning of the word *prerogative* and its application to the washing of the saints' feet.

4. What are some practices in your church that an unchurched person might think of as strange or odd?

5. What do you think are some of the main reasons people are reluctant to practice feet washing in church?

6. What role do you think embarrassment plays in some people's reluctance to practice the washing of feet? If you were convinced that Jesus commanded the literal washing of feet, would you be embarrassed by it?

7. Have you ever experienced anything that at first seemed odd to you but that you later became accustomed to?

CHAPTER TWO

"What Is an Ordinance?"

1. What is the main difference between sacraments and ordinances?

2. Do Free Will Baptists believe in ordinances or sacraments? Why?

3. What is the difference between something (a) *memorializing* or *symbolizing* Christ and His gospel and (b) *conveying* or *transmitting* divine grace?

4. Which group influenced our Free Will Baptist forefathers, the English General Baptists, in their view of ordinances: Mennonites or Lutherans?

5. Contemplate how you have defined *ordinance* in the past. How does it compare to these historical views?

6. Does the Bible explicitly define *ordinance*? If so, in what passages?

7. Must something symbolize Christ's death to be an ordinance? Why or why not?

8. Do you think some Christians too quickly dismiss feet washing as an ordinance because it does not measure up to an arbitrary definition of *ordinance*?

CHAPTER THREE

"Appointed by Christ for Literal Perpetuation"

1. Re-read John 13:2-17. What might suggest to the reader that Jesus is not merely observing ordinary social custom—not just washing the disciples' feet to get them clean?

2. What do you think might be the significance of the painstaking, ceremonious way that Jesus moves through this act?

3. What does the word *ought* mean in John 13:14? How does this usage relate to our modern usage of the word?

4. Re-read Matthew 26:26, 27; 28:19, 20; Mark 14:22; 16:16; Luke 22:19; John 13:7, 12, 14, 15, 17. Do these passages indicate a clearer, more direct command for baptism and the Lord's Supper than they do for feet washing? If so, how?

5. What is the Quaker argument regarding baptism, the Lord's Supper, and feet washing, and how does it relate to the main point of this chapter?

6. Do you think the literal practice of feet washing is easier to dismiss if humility is the only thing the gospel account symbolizes?

7. If the washing of the saints' feet symbolized the incarnation of Christ and our sanctification, do you think it could be observed by mere daily humble acts?

CHAPTER FOUR

"The Symbolism of Feet Washing"

1. Must feet washing "typify Christ" to qualify as an ordinance? Why or why not?

2. In what way is the washing of the saints' feet a "two-pronged" ordinance?

3. Re-read Matthew 22:37-39. How does feet washing symbolize Jesus' thoughts in this passage?

4. Does modern individualism encourage the practice of feet washing?

5. How do Howard Dorgan's story and Michael Card's song illustrate feet washing as it relates to interpersonal reconciliation?

6. Have you ever had—or ever heard of—experiences of reconciliation and emotional or spiritual healing that were tied to the experience of feet washing?

7. Re-read Philippians 2:6-8. Does the washing of the saints' feet remind you of the truths of this passage? How?

8. How does feet washing symbolize daily cleansing from sin? How does John 13:10, 11 help us understand this?

CHAPTER FIVE

"Feet Washing Outside the Gospels"

1. Discuss some commands or practices in the New Testament that are not mentioned outside the Gospels.

2. What is the context of Paul's discussion of the Lord's Supper in 1 Corinthians, and how is this relevant to the idea that something must be mentioned in the epistles to qualify as an ordinance?

3. What are the main reasons the widows' "washing the saints' feet" in 1 Timothy 5:9, 10 is not a mere description of hospitality?

4. What did the church father Ambrose of Milan say about the church at Rome with regard to the washing of feet?

5. Re-read the quotations from Ambrose. Does he tie feet washing to cleansing from sin or sanctification? What else does he suggest it symbolizes?

6. Re-read the passages from Augustine. Does he think it is better to wash feet "with the hand" or "in heart"?

7. What is the significance of these thoughts of the church fathers for the practice of feet washing?

CHAPTER SIX

"Why the Lord's Supper and Feet Washing Go Together"

1. What does this chapter describe as three types of "ritual ordinances"?

2. What does baptism symbolize?

3. How does the Lord's Supper relate to Christ's death and our death to sin? How does it relate to justification?

4. How does feet washing relate to Christ's resurrection and our resurrection to newness of life? How does it relate to sanctification?

5. Study the table on p. 86 and discuss it. How do the concepts of objective/subjective and vertical/horizontal relate to the washing of the saints' feet?

FOR FURTHER READING

General

Dorgan, Howard. *Giving Glory to God in Appalachia: Worship Practices of Six Baptist Subdenominations*. Knoxville: The University of Tennessee Press, 1987.

Edgington, Allen. "Footwashing as an Ordinance," *Grace Theological Journal* 6/2: 1985.

Gillespie, Paul F., ed., *Foxfire 7*. Garden City: Anchor/Doubleday, 1982.

Hardon, John A. *The Catholic Catechism: A Contemporary Catechism of the Teachings of the Catholic Church*. Garden City: Doubleday, 1975.

Plaster, David R. *Ordinances: What Are They?* Winona Lake, Ind.: BMH, 1985.

Powers, Jeanne Audrey. *Ritual in a New Day: An Invitation* [a study of the Alternate Rituals Project of the Section on Worship of the Board of Discipleship of the United Methodist Church]. Nashville: Abingdon, 1976.

Schaff, Philip. *A History of the Christian Church*, vols. 3 and 5. Grand Rapids: Eerdmans, 1950 [1910] and 1952 [1907].

Shultz, Joseph R. *The Soul of the Symbols: A Theological Study of Holy Communion*. Grand Rapids: Eerdmans, 1966.

Thomas, John Christopher. *Footwashing in John 13 and the Johannine Community*. Sheffield, England: University of Sheffield Academic Press, 1991.

Free Will Baptist History and Practice

An Abstract of the Former Articles of Faith Confessed by the Original Baptist Church Holding the Doctrine of General Provision. With a Proper Code of Discipline for the Future Government of the Church (Newbern, N.C.: Salmon Hall, 1813, authorized 1812), Repr. J. Matthew Pinson, *A Free Will Baptist Handbook: Heritage, Beliefs, and Ministries*.

Griffin, J. C. *The Upper Room Ought*. Ayden, N.C.: Free Will Baptist Press, 1927.

Hearn, Rufus K., Joseph S. Bell, and Jesse Randolph. *Zion's Hymns: For the Use of the Original Free-Will Baptist Church of North Carolina, and for the Saints of All Denominations*. Pikeville, N.C. Elder Daniel Davis, 1854.

Hinnant, R. N., J. C. Griffin, J. O. Fort, and I. J. Blackwelder, eds., *Free Will Baptist Hymnal: Hymns and Gospel Songs for Every Phase of Worship*. Ayden, N.C.: Free Will Baptist Press and Nashville, Tenn.: National Association of Free Will Baptists, 1958.

Jeffrey, William. *The Whole Faith of Man: Being the Gospel Declared in Plainness, As It Is in Jesus*. London: Francis Smith, 1659.

Picirilli, Robert E. *Church Ordinances and Government*. Nashville: Randall House, 1973.

Pinson, J. Matthew. *A Free Will Baptist Handbook: Heritage, Beliefs, and Ministries*. Nashville: Randall House, 1998.

_____. "Toward a Theology of the Ordinances with Special Reference to Feet Washing," *Integrity: A Journal of Christian Thought*, Summer 2000, pp. 67-87.

Rejoice: The Free Will Baptist Hymn Book. Antioch, Tenn.: Executive Office, National Association of Free Will Baptists, 1988.

A Treatise of the Faith and Practices of the National Association of Free Will Baptists. Antioch, Tenn.: Executive Office, National Association of Free Will Baptists, rev. 1996.

Ordinances and Sacraments

Barclay, Robert. *An Apology for the True Christian Divinity: Being an Explanation and Vindication of the Principles and Doctrines of the People Called Quakers*, 8th ed. New York: Samuel Wood and Sons, 1827.

The Book of Common Prayer. New York: James Pott and Company, 1892.

Conner, W. T. *Christian Doctrine*. Nashville: Broadman, 1937.

Criswell, W. A. *The Doctrine of the Church*. Nashville: Convention, 1980.

Dagg, John Leadley. *A Treatise of Church Order*, 1858. Repr. Harrisonburg, Va.: Gano, 1990.

Hovey, Alvah. *Manual of Systematic Theology and Christian Ethics.* Philadelphia: American Baptist Publication Society, 1877.

Johnson, E. H., and Henry G. Weston. *An Outline of Systematic Theology and of Ecclesiology.* Philadelphia: American Baptist Publication Society, 1895.

Lumpkin, William L., ed. *Baptist Confessions of Faith.* Valley Forge, Pa.: Judson, 1969.

Luther, Martin. "The Short Catechism, 1529," in Henry Bettenson, ed., *Documents of the Christian Church.* New York: Oxford University Press, 1947.

Macquarrie, John. "Baptism, Confirmation, Eucharist," in *Signs of Faith, Hope, and Love: The Christian Sacraments Today.* San Francisco: Collins Liturgical, 1988.

Strong, Augustus Hopkins. *Systematic Theology.* Philadelphia: Judson, 1907.

Sykes, Stephen W. "The Sacraments," in *Christian Theology: An Introduction to Its Traditions and Tasks.* Peter C. Hodgson and Robert H. King, eds. Philadelphia: Fortress, 1982.

Commentaries

Barrett, C. K. *The Pastoral Epistles.* Oxford: Clarendon, 1963.

Borchert, Gerald L. *John 12-21* in the *New American Commentary.* Nashville: Broadman & Holman, 2002.

Brown, Raymond E. *The Gospel According to John.* 2 vols; Garden City: Doubleday, 1966-70.

Bruce, F. F. *The Gospel of John.* Grand Rapids: Eerdmans, 1983.

Calvin, John. *Commentary on the Gospel According to John.* Trans. W. Pringle. Grand Rapids: Eerdmans, 1949.

Carson, D. A. *The Gospel According to John* in the *Pillar New Testament Commentary.* Grand Rapids: Eerdmans, 1991.

Dodd, C. H. *The Interpretation of the Fourth Gospel.* Cambridge: Cambridge University Press, 1953.

Edwards, Mark. *John* in the *Blackwell Bible Commentaries.* Oxford, England: Blackwell, 2004.

Forlines, F. Leroy. *Romans* in the *Randall House Bible Commentary.* Nashville: Randall House, 1987.

Gill, John. *An Exposition of the Old and New Testaments.* Paris, Ark.: Baptist Standard Bearer, 1989.

Henry, Matthew. *Commentary on the Whole Bible.* Peabody, Mass.: Hendrickson, 1991.

Hunter, A. M. *The Gospel According to John* in the *Cambridge Bible Commentaries on the New Testament.* Cambridge, England: Cambridge University Press, 1965.

Jamieson, Robert., A. R. Fausset, David Brown. *A Commentary, Critical and Explanatory, on the Old and New Testaments.* Hartford: S. S. Scranton, n.d..

Kent, Homer. *The Pastoral Epistles.* Chicago: Moody, 1958.

Lenski, R. C. H., *St. John's Gospel.* Columbus: Lutheran Book Concern, 1942.

Michaels, J. Ramsey. *John* in the *Harper Good News Commentary.* New York: Harper & Row, 1984.

Morris, Leon. *The Gospel of John* in the *New International Commentary on the New Testament.* Grand Rapids: Eerdmans, 1995.

Outlaw, Stanley. *1 Timothy* in the *Randall House Bible Commentary.* Nashville: Randall House, 1990.

Picirilli, Robert, ed., *John* in the *Randall House Bible Commentary.* Nashville: Randall House, 1989.

Ryan, Joseph F. *That You May Believe: Studies in the Gospel of John.* Wheaton, Ill.: Crossway, 2003.

Talbert, Charles H. *Reading John: A Literary and Theological Commentary on the Fourth Gospel and the Johannine Epistles.* New York: Crossroad, 1992.

INDEX

SCRIPTURE INDEX

NAME INDEX

ABOUT THE AUTHOR

 J. Matthew Pinson is president of Free Will Baptist Bible College in Nashville, Tennessee. Before his current position, he labored as a pastor, teacher, and writer in Alabama, Connecticut, and Georgia. A native of Pensacola, Florida, Mr. Pinson holds degrees from Yale University and the University of West Florida and is currently completing a doctorate at Vanderbilt University. He is author of another Randall House book entitled *A Free Will Baptist Handbook: Heritage, Beliefs, and Ministries*. He lives with his wife, Melinda, and their children, Anna and Matthew, in Nashville.

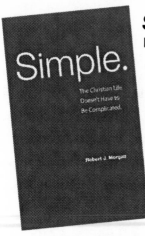

Also from
RANDALL HOUSE PUBLICATIONS.

Randall House Publications Bible Commentary Series

Hebrews—W. Stanley Outlaw
ISBN 0892655143 $29.99

Mark—Robert E. Picirilli
ISBN 0892655143 $29.99

John—Jack W. Stallings
ISBN 0892655143 $29.99

Romans—F. Leroy Forlines
ISBN 0892655143 $29.99

1 & 2 Corinthians—Robert E. Picirilli
ISBN 0892655143 $29.99

Galatians & Colossians—Marberry, Picirilli, and Ellis
ISBN 0892655143 $29.99

1 Thessalonians & Philemon—Picirilli, Outlaw, and Ellis
ISBN 0892655143 $29.99

James, 1 & 2 Peter, Jude—Harrison and Picirilli
ISBN 0892655143 $29.99

*Randall House Publications Bible Commentary
Eight Volume Set* **$199.99**

Rejoice: The Free Will Baptist Hymn Book

The National Association of Free Will Baptists

There is no substitute for the *Free Will Baptist Hymn Book REJOICE!* It reflects the heritage and distinctives of the denomination's love for music and worship. With 728 songs and responsive readings, all indexed multiple ways to assist you in preparing a service that glorifies God.

Call 1-800-877-7030 for custom-color price and color charts.

9990115397 6x9 Black (3-ring binder only, hymnal pages sold separately) - $9.99
0892657545 Sky Blue shaped notes (cloth bound) - $13.99
0892657448 NEW COLOR Royal Blue round notes (cloth bound) - $13.99
089265743X Sky Blue round notes (cloth bound) - $13.99
0892657618 Cardinal Red round notes (cloth bound) - $13.99
0892657553 Spring Green round notes (cloth bound) - $13.99
0892655038 Accompanist (loose leaf sheets) round notes - $16.99
0892655046 Accompanist (loose leaf sheets) shaped notes - $16.99

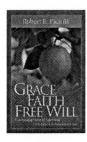

Grace, Faith, Free Will
Robert E. Picirilli

Though he presents both classic Calvinism and Arminianism in order to help readers intelligently decide for themselves, Dr. Picirilli unashamedly advocates a very specific form of Arminianism as the best resolution of the tensions between the two doctrinal positions. In what he calls "Reformation Arminianism," Picirilli reclaims the original views of Arminius and his defenders.

ISBN 0892656484 - $19.99

The Quest For Truth: Answering Life's Inescapable Questions
F. Leroy Forlines

This invaluable tool discusses profound truths that apply to every facet of life. Forlines asserts that biblical truth should be make applicable to the total personality. These "inescapable questions of life" are answered from the standard of God's authoritative Word.

ISBN 0892659629 paperback - $29.99
ISBN 0892658649 hardback - $34.99

Randall House Ministers Manual
& New Testament

The *Randall House Ministers Manual* is an essential resource for any minister. The manual includes the entire New Testament and Psalms text as well as sample wedding services, funeral services, baby dedications, and much more.

ISBN 0892655402 - $17.99

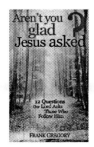

Aren't You Glad Jesus Asked?
12 Questions Our Lord Asks Those Who Follow Him
Frank Gregory

By focusing on 12 questions Jesus asked His disciples, this Bible study points out the importance and responsibility of evangelism in every believer's life.

ISBN 0892655410 Paperback - $9.99

To order visit *www.RandallHouse.com* or call 1-800-877-7030.

"Mr. Pinson brings both a scholarly and pastoral perspective to this important study of feet washing, a practice of the early church that was once more commonly observed among Baptists and other Christians than it is today. This book relates feet washing to the central doctrine of the Christian faith, the Incarnation, as well as to the value of humility and community in Christian discipleship. A first-rate study by a superb Baptist theologian!"

Timothy George
Dean, Beeson Divinity School of Samford University
Executive Editor, *Christianity Today*

"With this work Matthew Pinson continues to give us sound biblical, ecclesiastical, and theological reasons for practicing feet washing as an ordinance. I found the book easy to read, and yet it stimulates serious thinking on a variety of subjects related to this traditional practice, including the depth of its meaning. I trust that the work will serve to solidify again this time-honored practice of our people—and numerous other branches of the Christian church, past and present."

Robert E. Picirilli
Professor Emeritus
Free Will Baptist Bible College

"The role and significance of foot washing in the life of the church appears to be experiencing a resurgence in practice amongst a variety of Christian groups. Matthew Pinson's fine volume makes a valuable contribution to the growing theological literature on this topic, not only for those within the Free Will Baptist tradition, but also for others interested in this topic. The integration of historical investigation with biblical, theological, and practical reflection makes this a most helpful volume indeed."

John Christopher Thomas
Clarence J. Abbott Professor of Biblical Studies
Church of God Theological Seminary

"*The Washing of the Saints' Feet* is a balanced presentation of a gospel ordinance Free Will Baptists have proclaimed and practiced for years without apology. J. Matthew Pinson uses Scripture, historical documentation, and common sense to build a strong case in support of our distinctive denominational teaching on this subject. This book can reshape the thinking of some and reinforce the convictions of others regarding this important yet often neglected practice."

Keith Burden
Executive Secretary
National Association of Free Will Baptists, Inc.

"It would seem that President Pinson has left little unsaid, unless he had wished to multiply comments from countless biblical scholars and ecclesiologists during two millennia of Christian history—which thankfully he has not. Over the years he has practiced faithfully, thought carefully, and read widely and well. Many of his readers will find his work convincing; all will find it profitable."

Robert G. Gardner
Senior Researcher in Baptist History
Tarver Library
Mercer University

"The practice of washing the saints' feet is a neglected treasure of the church (and a command of Christ!) that we desperately need to recover today. This book by Pinson provides the instruction, encouragement, and guidance necessary to that recovery. His treatment is biblical, historical, and pastorally wise; it is accessible and instructive both to those who have observed this command of Christ and those who have never even thought about it. This book and the practice that it commends should be embraced by all who seek a deeper understanding of God's grace and of the call of Christian discipleship."

Jonathan R. Wilson
Pioneer McDonald Professor of Theology
Carey Theological College

Printed in the United States
80416LV00001B/52-150